THE Garlic COOKBOOK

THE
Garlic
COOKBOOK

LORNA RHODES

a Salamander book
Published by Salamander Books Limited
LONDON

A SALAMANDER BOOK

Published by Salamander Books Ltd
129-137 York Way
London N7 9LG
United Kingdom

1 3 5 7 9 8 6 4 2

ISBN 0 86101 779 X

All correspondence concerning the content of this volume should be addressed to
Salamander Books Ltd.

CREDITS
COMMISSIONING EDITOR: *Will Steeds*
EDITOR: *Miranda Spicer*
DESIGN: *The Design Revolution, Brighton*
PHOTOGRAPHER: *Simon Butcher*
HOME ECONOMIST: *Lorna Rhodes*
STYLIST: *Hilary Guy*
COLOUR SEPARATION: *P & W Graphics*

Printed in Singapore

ACKNOWLEDGMENTS
The publishers wish to thank
Colin Boswell, Mersley Farms, Newchurch, Sandown, Isle of Wight
for his help and use of the photograph on page 10; and
David Roser of The Garlic Research Bureau.

ABOUT THE INGREDIENTS
When making any of the recipes in this book, you should follow either the metric or the
imperial measures, as these are not interchangeable.
As seasoning is a matter of personal taste, salt and pepper are not
necessarily listed in the ingredients.
Try to obtain the best quality fresh produce.

CONTENTS

AUTHOR'S INTRODUCTION

I cannot imagine cooking without garlic as it transforms the taste of the simplest food to something really delicious. No other plant can perform this miracle of making bread, vegetables or meat so tasty. The cuisines in every part of the world make use of garlic in varying quantities, either subtly, so it hardly seems to be there, or in copious quantities, which surprisingly do not overpower the flavour of the food. Garlic can be used very successfully in large quantities. When it is prepared, either by slow cooking in oil or by boiling in water, the cloves are transformed into soft, sweet, nuggets.

Garlic is inspirational. It conjures up a vision of appetizing food full of flavour, enjoyed in the company of friends and family, with wine and conversation flowing. It is reminiscent of eating together around the table at a leisurely pace, with time to savour the food – one of life's greatest pleasures.

When I studied Home Economics in the late 1960s, I was armed with my favourite (and for me the best) cookery book ever, *French Provincial Cooking* by Elizabeth David. What an influence this book had on me and my developing cookery talents! And it was also my introduction to cooking with garlic. Suddenly I found myself cooking garlic-laden, Mediterranean-style food as my parents had never known, much to the pleasure of my flat mates. My love of garlic has never faltered. Whilst experimenting with Middle Eastern, Indian, Chinese and Thai cookery over the years, I have continued to be drawn to the rich and gutsy flavours of the Mediterranean. It is this love of garlic-enriched foods which brought me to write this book. But what a difficult task to choose recipes – there are so many!

Adding garlic to the simplest ingredients elevates them from the ordinary and prevents food becoming boring and tasteless. If you are lucky enough to obtain green garlic, which resembles leeks with fat bulbs, it's certainly worth using for its subtle flavour. Garlic is available throughout the year from different countries. Its appearance varies, from the size of the bulb, to the colour of the skin. You may prefer to buy the attractive braids, especially if you use garlic frequently. Smoked garlic, with its golden skin, is more unusual and has a gentle garlic flavour.

For years the French and Italians have trusted garlic to give their cooking the distinctive flavour that is appreciated and copied all over the world. Both the British and Americans can still be inhibited about using the pungent bulb, but with an increasing love of foreign foods have come to appreciate its value. Mediterranean food has become a major influence on many diets with, for example, quick-cooking pasta dishes becoming family favourites. The whole ethos of the Mediterranean diet is now being recognized as beneficial to health, so it is no wonder that garlic is becoming an everyday ingredient in households across the globe.

Lorna Rhodes

INTRODUCTION

Since ancient times, people around the world have had a long and passionate relationship with garlic. As long ago as 5000 BC clay models of garlic bulbs were buried with Egyptians in their tombs and more than 3000 years later Tutankhamun was buried with the real thing.

The countries of both the Greek and Roman Empires made wide use of garlic, and the Old Testament tells us that the Israelites in the wilderness remembered: . . . "the fish, which we did eat freely; the cucumbers, and the melons, and the leeks, and the onions, and the garlick" (Numbers 11:5). The English name comes from the Anglo-Saxon 'Gar-Leac' or Spear Plant, referring to the spear-shaped leaves.

The smell of garlic has been commented on profusely. Our modern-day enjoyment of this pungent bulb should not be denied through fear of comparison with 16th century Henry VI of France who chewed garlic and had "a breath that would fell an ox at twenty paces". Nevertheless, the smell of garlic has meant that the whims of polite society, whether Roman or Victorian,

ABOVE: *Garlic is widely used in the cuisines of countries bordering the Mediterranean.*

deemed garlic occasionally unfashionable. Mrs. Beeton wrote:

"The smell of this plant is generally considered offensive. It was in greater repute with our ancestors than it is with ourselves, although it is still used today as a seasoning or herb." This feeling was shared across the Atlantic in the USA where it was considered, alongside olive oil, to be the most unpopular taste.

Garlic has been valued throughout history as a medicine as well as a food. It has held a reputation at one time or another as a remedy for virtually every illness – it has even been recommended as an aphrodisiac and a discourager of vampires. There can be little doubt that its more mainstream medicinal uses, both historically and in the present day, have proved both effective and beneficial.

Garlic's popularity is enjoying a revival. Nowadays, garlic festivals are held wherever it is grown commercially, usually in spring and early summer when the new season's crop comes in. In England, the Isle of Wight festival is at Newchurch in August, where the air is heavy with the aroma of garlic. Similar festivals occur in France and Spain, but in the USA there is the Gilroy festival which attracts some 100,000 visitors. The Californian farming town calls itself 'the world's garlic capital'. In both Newchurch and Gilroy the festival atmosphere is a mixture of a country fair, a gourmet food festival and a late 1960s pop festival. There is plenty of opportunity to participate in tastings.

Countries where garlic is grown as an agricultural crop use it in abundance and appreciate its potency. Travel to the Mediterranean has re-emphasised garlic's influence and has led to a resurgence in interest in garlicky food in the home countries of returning holidaymakers. The European, Central American and South American immigrants to the USA have brought garlic with them to expand and enliven 'American' cooking. Throughout history, garlic has crossed centuries and borders, allowing us to enjoy its special flavour and qualities.

GARLIC AND HEALTH

Herbalists have used garlic since 1500 BC. From China, Greece, Egypt and the ancient kingdoms of Babylon, Sumeria and Mesopotamia come complex recipes for all manner of diseases and health problems. All of these writings extol garlic as the king of medicinal plants as well as making much of its virtues as a key ingredient in daily diet. But do these age-old stories of garlic's medicinal magic hold up under the rigorous scrutiny of science and medicine today?

Until very recently, scientists and researchers were sceptical about the diseases that garlic claimed to treat. The list includes heart and arterial diseases; cholesterol control; reduction in internal blood clotting; prevention and cure of bacterial infections from Salmonella and Listeria organisms; anti-fungal activities against Candida species and so on. But is garlic really a cure-all?

Current rigorous scientific analysis and clinical research in hospitals and universities is clearly indicating that it does have a major and beneficial effect, both in remedying and preventing such key health problems. Garlic's secret is that inside each clove, contained in each of the individual cells, are two very important materials which are quite separate from one another in the growing plant. But the moment the clove is crushed or sliced these materials are brought together and a master material called allicin is created. The smell of fresh-cut garlic is the sign that allicin has been made. Allicin quickly breaks down when exposed to the air and through the heat of cooking, into over 70 different sulphur-bearing compounds. Many of these have specific effects on the body and this is why garlic is able to help with so many separate health problems.

In the late 1970s, a massive survey of the diets of 17

countries was carried out to establish which foods might explain the enormous differences between the incidences of cardio-vascular diseases in Western countries in comparison with the low incidences in Mediterranean countries. The conclusion was that eating raw or cooked garlic and onions (in daily diet) was responsible – with the possible additional benefits of drinking a glass or two of red wine. The day-to-day consumption of garlic is now known to have major protective effects.

So garlic can protect the arteries against fatty blockages; lower cholesterol levels if they are too high; help to prevent internal clots; kill stomach bugs; help with the symptoms of colds and 'flu' and even stop mosquitoes from biting, because of the unpalatable sulphur molecules on the skin when garlic is taken regularly!

Garlic adds zest and flavour to food, and research indicates that if it is consumed regularly it may lead to improved general health.

THE CULTIVATION OF GARLIC

Garlic, *Allium sativum*, is part of the lily family that also includes onion, shallots, leeks, and chives. Garlic does not develop its full flavour until the bulbs have been allowed to dry and the outer layers appear papery and flaky. Single garlic cloves are planted annually in November. These are referred to as seed, by growers. Each bulb is made up of eight to ten cloves; the bulbs are divided into individual cloves which are planted. In the spring the plants produce long pointed leaves known as garlic shoots. They can sometimes be found in specialist greengrocers, but if you grow your own, all the better. They can be used in salads or added to egg dishes and sauces and have a mild, fresh garlic flavour. Slightly older, firmer shoots can be used in Chinese cooking.

Green garlic is available at the start of the season; again it can be found in some greengrocers or if you have grown your own, lift a month before harvesting. 'Green' or 'wet' garlic is the fresh white heads with green stems and juicy cloves, which have a mild flavour; its overall appearance is more like a leek. Its prized flavour is used in place of leeks or onions in soups, or cooked in soufflés. Green garlic will not keep for more than two or three weeks, whereas the dried heads keep for months.

At the beginning of July, the bulbs have finished swelling and the stems begin to dry out. When the bulbs are harvested the stalks are left on and they are laid out in rows in the fields to dry in the sun. During this drying or curing time the cloves remain plump and juicy and the outer skin becomes flaky. The roots are then trimmed and the stems are snipped or plaited into a braid. Between July and December the garlic comes from the northern hemisphere, from February onwards the new crop comes from the southern hemisphere. There are differences in the shape, size and flavour, depending on where it is grown and the colour, which is either white, red, purple or pink.

Garlic needs plenty of sunshine, and grows well in warm countries, however English garlic is also available. It is grown on the Isle of Wight, can now be found in most supermarkets and has a good shelf life. French garlic from the Mediterranean areas of south-west France and Provence has big juicy cloves and an excellent flavour, but does not keep well. Look out for the famous **Rose de Lautrec**, which is pink garlic from Lautrec. The garlic most commonly available during winter months is **Spanish Morado**, which has large cloves and keeps well. **Venetian Italian** garlic from the Po valley is a white dense bulb that also keeps well.

Chinese garlic has a symmetrical bulb in a thin purply or silver skin and has little flavour. Elephant garlic which has a diameter of 7.5-10 cm (3-4 inches) is not a true garlic, it originates from south-east Asia and lacks the familiar strong flavour.

ABOVE: Newly harvested Isle of Wight garlic.

Oak-smoked garlic is now available in some supermarkets. The garlic is smoked in a conventional smokehouse in a cold smoking process which takes up to 48 hours. The smoked bulbs are milder, give a hint of smoke and are supposed not to have an aftertaste.

GROW YOUR OWN GARLIC

There is a garlic which has been best adapted to the UK climate (see Acknowledgements, page 4, for supplier). Start with a healthy looking bulb with fat cloves. Separate the cloves and plant them individually, pointed end up, about 10 cm (4 inches) apart and 5 cm (2 inches), deep, in autumn or early spring. They should be ready to harvest in July or August.

Select the best bulbs and re-plant them in the autumn for bigger bulbs the next summer. To dry, clean off the soil from the bulbs and trim the roots. Put them in a sunny place where the air can circulate and leave for two to three weeks until the stems are very dry. If it rains, bring them inside. Trim the stems and either bunch together or plait. Store in a cool, dry dark place.

COOKING WITH GARLIC

The famous cook Marcel Boulestin said:

"It is not an exaggeration to find that happiness and health is found where a lot of garlic is used in the kitchen."

In countries where garlic is grown, the local recipes include an abundance of garlic. Whole heads of garlic, roasted until they are soft and sweet, is a common sight. How much garlic is put in a dish is entirely a matter of taste, but the recipes in this book celebrate the use of lots of garlic.

The simplest way to peel a clove of garlic is to crush it beneath the blade of a heavy knife. There are some who swear by their garlic press and others who claim that it makes the fresh garlic taste bitter. The garlic press will produce a stronger garlic flavour. Many chefs prefer to dice lightly rather than crush it. To hand crush, remove the skin, take a little salt and either chop the garlic or mash with the flat blade of the knife, or mash in a pestle with a mortar. The salt will absorb the juices and make it easier to scoop the tiny garlic pieces off the board (it is advisable to keep a tiny wooden board solely for this purpose). Remember to use the salt as part of the seasoning to the dish. Alternatively, peel the skin off with a sharp knife, then cut the cloves into slices or slivers, or look out for a useful gadget which slices the cloves easily.

Whole cloves of garlic added to a dish impart less flavour than crushed or chopped ones. When boiling vegetables, add whole peeled cloves to the water to impart a subtle aroma. When roasting foods, add whole cloves, peeled or unpeeled; they can be served and mashed on the plate to be eaten with the meat or vegetables. For dishes that require a less pronounced garlic flavour, poach the cloves for a few minutes in water to remove the strong pungency. Take this a step further and poach until tender, then press through a sieve to make a mild, creamy purée. This purée appears in recipes in this book, but also try adding it to soups, sauces and dips.

There are many ways in which the flavour of garlic can be introduced to a dish without incorporating it into the food. Dressings can be infused with the flavour of garlic by adding crushed or chopped garlic to the mixture, then straining before use. Alternatively, rub the cut side of a clove of garlic around the salad bowl before adding the ingredients. For hot dishes, heat some garlic in the oil or butter to flavour it, but remove the garlic before adding other ingredients. Take care not to burn it – it will cook in seconds in hot oil or butter. In some recipes it is cooked very gently, in others it is allowed to turn golden, but never too brown, or it will taste bitter.

Roasted whole heads of garlic can be cooked around a joint; allowing one head per person. The inside becomes soft and tastes sweet and nutty, and can be squeezed from the skins and eaten with the meat and vegetables. Roast whole heads of garlic and use the purée in sauces or spread on toast. Special earthenware garlic roasters are now available to cook one or more heads at a time. Alternatively wrap the heads loosely in foil, drizzle with oil and bake in a moderately hot oven until soft. Slicing the top off the bulb before cooking makes it easier to squeeze out the purée once cooked. Garlic wrapped in foil can also be roasted on a barbecue.

HINTS AND TIPS

• Add peeled whole cloves of garlic to a jar of oil, refrigerate and keep for 2-3 days before using. Brush on foods before they are grilled or sautéed.

• Add peeled cloves of garlic to white wine vinegar, and keep for 2-3 days before using in salad dressings.
• Bury 3 peeled and pressed cloves in half a cup of sea salt. Leave for a few days in a screw-topped jar. Remove garlic and use the salt as a seasoning.
• Make garlic purée by putting peeled cloves in a blender or food processor, add some olive oil and work until smooth. Store in a screw-topped jar for up to 5 days in the refrigerator. For a milder flavour, drain boiled garlic, either mash it with a fork or sieve it. It can be stored in a glass jar under a layer of olive oil, and will keep for 5 days in the refrigerator. Spread it on toast, add it to soups and sauces, stir it in to gravies, add it to vegetable purées or mashed potatoes.
• Peel 4 heads of garlic. Place in a glass jar with 4-6 small red chillies. Heat 300 ml (10 fl oz) cider vinegar with 15 ml (1 tbsp) sugar and 10 ml (2 tsp) salt. Cool, then pour over the garlic, seal and leave for 1 week.
• Peel 225 g (8 oz) garlic cloves, put in a pan and add enough oil to cover. Cook over medium heat for 20 minutes until tender. Cool, then pack in a jar. Keep it in the refrigerator and use within 5 days. Use on pizzas and add to pasta.
• Store a string of garlic in a cool dry place, not in a warm, steamy kitchen. Pull a head off as required and break open to release the cloves. Strings or braids of garlic are a good buy if you use lots of garlic; otherwise buy smaller quantities and store in an earthenware garlic cellar, which allows the air to circulate and protects the garlic from the light.
• If the garlic has sprouted, slice each clove in half, remove and discard the green shoot (the flavour of sprouted garlic can be bitter).

RIGHT: Left to right: (back row) garlic and thyme olive oil; garlic in white wine vinegar; earthenware garlic cellars; (front row) garlic roaster; garlic purée; roasted garlic in oil; minced garlic; garlic and chillies in cider vinegar.

STARTERS

Begin a meal with a garlic-flavoured dish guaranteed to whet the appetite. For an informal starter with a rich taste of garlic try Roasted Garlic and Avocado Dip. For a dinner party, there are smoked salmon rolls filled with a creamy mousse.

AIOLI WITH CRUDITÉS

6 *cloves* GARLIC, PEELED
2 EGG YOLKS
5 *ml (1 tsp)* DIJON MUSTARD
150 *ml (5 fl oz)* OLIVE OIL
150 *ml 5 fl oz)* GROUNDNUT OIL
10 *ml (2 tsp)* LEMON JUICE

Crudités
PREPARED RAW VEGETABLES E.G. CARROTS,
CELERY STICKS, RADISHES

Ensure the ingredients for the aioli are at room temperature, then put the garlic, egg yolks and mustard in a blender or food processor. With the motor running add the oils a few drops at a time until the mixture starts to thicken. Increase the flow of oil until it is all incorporated then beat in the lemon juice. Season with salt and pepper. Transfer to a bowl, cover and chill. Prepare a selection of colourful fresh crudités to serve with the aioli.   SERVES 4-6

AUBERGINE ROLLS WITH GARLIC TOMATO SAUCE

Sauce
30 *ml (2 tbsp)* OLIVE OIL
3 *cloves* GARLIC, CRUSHED
450 *g (1 lb)* RIPE PLUM TOMATOES, SKINNED
AND CHOPPED
2.5 *ml (½ tsp)* DRIED BASIL
30 *ml (2 tbsp)* DRY WHITE WINE

Aubergine rolls
2 x 225 *g (8 oz)* AUBERGINES
90 *ml (6 tbsp)* OLIVE OIL
150 *g (5 oz)* SOFT MILD GOAT'S CHEESE
2 TOMATOES, SKINNED AND CHOPPED
a few BASIL LEAVES, SHREDDED
flakes PARMESAN CHEESE, TO GARNISH

To make the sauce, simmer all the ingredients together for 20 minutes. Sieve, season and set aside.

Cut the aubergines lengthways into 8, 0.5cm (¼ inch) slices. Place in a large, flat colander, sprinkle with salt and leave to drain for 30 minutes. Rinse. Pat dry. Heat the oven to 190°C (375°F/Gas mark 5). Heat 30 ml (2 tbsp) oil in a frying pan, add a layer of aubergine and cook on each side until just golden. Drain on kitchen paper. Repeat with more oil and slices. When cooked, spread the goat's cheese on the aubergine slices, top with tomato and add some basil. Roll up. Place in an ovenproof dish and bake for 15-20 minutes. Garnish and serve with a pool of warm tomato sauce.   SERVES 4

TOP: Aioli with Crudités
BOTTOM: Aubergine Rolls with Garlic Tomato Sauce

GARLICKY SALMON KEBABS

❦

Eight small bamboo skewers are needed for these kebabs.

550 g (1¼ lb) SALMON FILLET, SKINNED
16 TIGER, OR OTHER LARGE PRAWNS, PEELED.
30 ml (2 tbsp) LIGHT SOY SAUCE
15 ml (1 tbsp) LIME JUICE
3 cloves GARLIC, FINELY CHOPPED
15 ml (1 tbsp) SUNFLOWER OIL
SHREDDED LETTUCE, TO SERVE

Soak the skewers in water before using, to prevent them burning. Cut the salmon into 2.5 cm (1 inch) cubes. Divide between the 8 bamboo skewers and thread onto them with the prawns. Pre-heat the grill. In a small bowl mix the soy sauce, lime juice, garlic and oil; use to brush the fish. Grill for 5-6 minutes, turning and brushing with sauce. Serve on a bed of shredded lettuce.

SERVES 4

SMOKED SALMON ROLLS WITH GARLIC MOUSSE

❦

Any left-over mousse can be served the next day with Melba toast.

175 ml (6 fl oz) BEEF CONSOMMÉ
5 ml (1 tsp) GELATINE
150 g (5 oz) SOFT CHEESE WITH GARLIC AND HERBS
60 ml (4 tbsp) FROMAGE FRAIS
1 clove GARLIC, CRUSHED
225 g (8 oz) SLICED SMOKED SALMON
LEMON SLICES AND PARSLEY, TO GARNISH

To make the garlic mousse, heat the consommé. Sprinkle the gelatine onto 15 ml (1 tbsp) of water and when spongy stir into the consommé to dissolve. Leave to cool. Pour into a blender or food processor. Add the cheese, fromage frais and garlic and blend until smooth. Pour into a bowl and chill until set.

Cut the slices of smoked salmon into lengths 6 cm (2½ inches) wide, to give 8 pieces. Place a tablespoonful of mousse at the end of each salmon piece and roll up. Serve 2 rolls per portion, garnished with lemon twists and parsley.

SERVES 4

PRAWNS IN GARLIC BUTTER

❦

115 g (4 oz) BUTTER, SOFTENED
4 cloves GARLIC, CRUSHED WITH SALT
1.25 ml (½ tsp) GRATED LEMON RIND
15 ml (1 tbsp) LEMON JUICE
45 ml (3 tbsp) CHOPPED PARSLEY
350 g (12 oz) TIGER PRAWNS OR OTHER LARGE PRAWNS, PEELED

Put the butter in a bowl. Add the garlic, lemon rind, juice and parsley. Season with pepper. Beat. Form into a roll on cling film. Wrap it and refrigerate.

Divide the prawns between 4 small ovenproof dishes. Slice the garlic butter and cover the prawns with it. Place under a hot grill and cook for 10 minutes, turning them after 5 minutes. Serve with French bread.

SERVES 4

TOP: Garlicky Salmon Kebabs, Smoked Salmon Rolls with Garlic Mousse
BOTTOM: Prawns in Garlic Butter

PORK AND GARLIC PÂTÉ

This pâté can be made in advance and kept for up to 4 days in the refrigerator.

55 g (2 oz) BUTTER OR POLYUNSATURATED MARGARINE
1 MEDIUM ONION, CHOPPED
55 g (2 oz) CELERY, CHOPPED
115 g (4 oz) MUSHROOMS, CHOPPED
115 g (4 oz) RINDLESS STREAKY BACON
4 fat cloves GARLIC, ROUGHLY CHOPPED
225 g (8 oz) PIGS, OR LAMBS LIVER
1 EGG, BEATEN
30 ml (2 tbsp) FRESH CHOPPED THYME OR
5 ml (1 tsp) DRIED THYME
30 ml (2 tbsp) FRESHLY CHOPPED PARSLEY
450 g (1 lb) MINCED PORK
30 ml (2 tbsp) BRANDY
2 BAY LEAVES

Melt the butter in a large frying pan. Add the onion, celery, mushrooms, bacon and garlic and cook for 8-10 minutes until softened. Cool. Transfer to the bowl of a blender or food processor.

Pre-heat the oven to 170°C (325°F/Gas mark 3). Roughly chop the liver, add to the blender with the egg. Purée. Transfer to a bowl. Add the herbs, pork and brandy. Season to taste. Stir until well blended. Spoon into a 1.1 litre (2 pint) ovenproof dish or loaf tin, top with 2 bay leaves. Cover with foil. Stand the dish in a roasting tin half full of water and cook for 2 hours. Cool. Place a weight on top of the pâté and refrigerate overnight.

Cut into slices and serve with toast or crusty bread.

SERVES 8

BRIE AND GARLIC FONDUE

6 cloves GARLIC, PEELED
120 ml (4 fl oz) DRY WHITE WINE
150 ml (¼ pint) SINGLE CREAM
350 g (12 oz) BRIE, RIND REMOVED
15 ml (1 tbsp) CORNFLOUR
30 ml (2 tbsp) BRANDY
CUBES OF FRENCH BREAD, TO SERVE

Put the garlic in a small pan, cover with water and simmer for 10 minutes until tender. Press the cloves through a sieve.

Pour the wine and cream into the fondue pot. Add the garlic purée and heat until bubbling. Cut the cheese into small pieces, add to the pot and stir until melted.

In a small bowl blend the cornflour and brandy. Add to the pan and continue to cook for 2 minutes, stirring constantly until thick and creamy. Serve with cubes of French bread.

SERVES 4

RIGHT: Pork and Garlic Pâté

ROASTED GARLIC AND AVOCADO DIP

1 large head GARLIC
15 ml (1 tbsp) OLIVE OIL
115 g (4 oz) MEDIUM-FAT CREAM CHEESE
150 ml (1/4 pint) SOUR CREAM
1 RIPE AVOCADO
15 ml (1 tbsp) LEMON JUICE
30 ml (2 tbsp) FINELY CHOPPED SPRING ONION
(OPTIONAL)

Pre-heat the oven to 200°C (400°F/Gas mark 6). Remove the papery outer skin from the head of garlic, without separating the cloves. Cut off 1.25 cm (1/4 inch) from the stem end. Place on foil, drizzle over the oil and loosely wrap. Alternatively, use a garlic roaster. Bake for 40 minutes, until the cloves are soft. Cool.

Squeeze the garlic to remove the cloves from the skin. Put in a blender or food processor with the cream cheese and soured cream. Purée until smooth. Scoop out the flesh from the avocado. Add to the cream and cheese mixture with the lemon juice and work again until just smooth. Season. Stir in the onion, if using.   SERVES 6

MUSHROOMS TRIFOLATI

The Italian way of cooking vegetables in olive oil, garlic and parsley is described as 'trifolati', where the name of this dish comes from.

90 ml (6 tbsp) OLIVE OIL
4 cloves GARLIC, FINELY CHOPPED
350 g (12 oz) CHESTNUT MUSHROOMS, SLICED
350 g (12 oz) CLOSED CUP MUSHROOMS, SLICED
45 ml (3 tbsp) CHOPPED PARSLEY

Heat the oil in a large frying pan over medium heat. Add the garlic and cook for a few seconds to release the aroma. Increase the heat, add the mushrooms and quickly turn so they evenly absorb the oil. Toss the mushrooms in the pan for 4-5 minutes until tender. Season. Stir in the parsley then turn into a dish. Cool. Serve at room temperature.   SERVES 6

BRUSCHETTA WITH TOMATOES

This Italian garlic bread uses olive oil instead of butter and the addition of tomatoes makes it a more substantial starter.

3 LARGE, VERY RIPE TOMATOES, SKINNED
1 CIABATTA LOAF OR FRENCH LOAF
3 large cloves GARLIC, PEELED
2.5 ml (1/2 tsp) SALT
60 ml (4 tbsp) EXTRA VIRGIN OLIVE OIL
1 SMALL RED ONION, CHOPPED,
SMALL BASIL LEAVES, TO GARNISH

Roughly chop the tomatoes. Cut the bread into diagonal slices, 1.25 cm (1/2 inch) thick. Mash the garlic with the salt to form a paste. Put in a bowl and mix with the olive oil. Toast the bread on both sides. Brush one side of each slice of bread with garlic mixture. Top with tomato onion and basil leaves. Serve immediately.   SERVES 4

TOP: Roasted Garlic and Avocado Dip
BOTTOM: Mushrooms Trifolati

SOUPS

Generous amounts of garlic are added to these soups, which range from a Provençal Pistou to Chinese Noodle Soup. Garlic Soup calls for smoked garlic which can be used to vary the flavour of all soups, but if this is not available use a head of dried or fresh garlic instead.

PISTOU

This hearty soup originates from Provence. It is given extra flavor by the addition of pistou sauce made with garlic, basil, olive oil and Parmesan cheese, which gives the soup its name.

30 ml (2 tbsp) OLIVE OIL
1 SMALL ONION, CHOPPED
3 cloves GARLIC, FINELY CHOPPED
2 SMALL LEEKS, THINLY SLICED
2 stalks CELERY, CHOPPED
1.2 litres (2 pints) CHICKEN OR VEGETABLE STOCK
175 g (6 oz) FRENCH GREEN BEANS, CUT INTO SHORT LENGTHS
2 SMALL COURGETTES, DICED
1 SMALL POTATO, DICED
225 g (8 oz) CAN CHOPPED TOMATOES
1 x 440 g (15 1/2 oz) CAN HARICOT BEANS, DRAINED
55 g (2 oz) SMALL PASTA SHAPES

Sauce
4 cloves GARLIC
LARGE BUNCH BASIL LEAVES
45 g (1 1/2 oz) PINE NUTS
45 g (3 tbsp) EXTRA VIRGIN OLIVE OIL
45 g (1 1/2 oz) FRESHLY GRATED PARMESAN CHEESE

For the soup, heat the oil in a large saucepan. Add the onion and cook until softened. Add the garlic, leeks and celery and cook for 2 minutes. Pour in the stock, add the rest of the vegetables and simmer for 15 minutes. Stir in the pasta and continue to cook for 10-15 minutes until the pasta is *al dente*. Season to taste.

While the soup is simmering, make the pistou sauce. Pound the garlic in a mortar until crushed, add the basil and pine nuts and pound to a paste. Alternatively, purée in a small blender or food processor. Mix in the oil, a little at a time. Finally, stir in the Parmesan. Serve with the pistou sauce swirled on top.   SERVES 6

RIGHT: Pistou

GARLIC SOUP

To garnish the soup, cut small shapes from 2 slices of white bread and fry in the residual garlic oil until golden. Dry on kitchen paper.

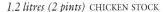

1 head OAK-SMOKED GARLIC
30 ml (2 tbsp) OLIVE OIL
45 g (1 1/2 oz) BUTTER
1 LARGE SPANISH ONION, FINELY CHOPPED
700 ml (1 1/4 pints) CHICKEN STOCK
115 g (4 oz) DAY-OLD CRUSTLESS WHITE BREAD
150 ml (1 1/4 pint) SINGLE CREAM
25 g (1 oz) GROUND ALMONDS, FINELY CHOPPED
CHOPPED PARSLEY OR CHIVES, TO GARNISH

Separate the garlic cloves, removing the papery skins. Heat the oil in a pan, add the garlic and cook for about 10-15 minutes until tender. Remove from the heat. Cool, then skin. Roughly chop the flesh. Melt the butter in a large saucepan, add the garlic and onion and cook over a low heat. Cover and cook for 10-15 minutes until the onion is soft. Pour in the stock, add the bread and simmer for 30 minutes. Transfer the soup to the bowl of a blender or food processor. Add the cream and almonds and blend until smooth. Garnish and serve. SERVES 4

CHINESE NOODLE SOUP

1.2 litres (2 pints) CHICKEN STOCK
2.5 cm (1 inch) FRESH GINGER, FINELY CHOPPED
4 cloves GARLIC, FINELY CHOPPED
75 g (3 oz) BUTTON MUSHROOMS, SLICED
15 ml (1 tbsp) FISH SAUCE
50 g (2 oz) RICE VERMICELLI
3 SPRING ONIONS, THINLY SLICED
15 ml (1 tbsp) SHREDDED FRESH CORIANDER LEAVES, TO GARNISH

Put the stock, ginger and garlic in a saucepan. Slowly bring to the boil. Add the mushrooms to the pan with fish sauce, and cover Simmer for 10 minutes.

Meanwhile, soak the noodles for 10 minutes. Drain the noodles, add to the soup and simmer for 3 minutes until cooked. Scatter the spring onions over the soup and garnish. SERVES 4

BEETROOT AND GARLIC SOUP

25 g (1 oz) BUTTER
1 SPANISH ONION, CHOPPED
115 g (4 oz) GARLIC
450 g (1 lb) BEETROOT, PEELED AND CUT INTO SMALL DICE
1 LARGE POTATO, PEELED AND DICED
900 ml (1 1/2 pints) VEGETABLE STOCK
CHOPPED PARSLEY, TO GARNISH
SOUR CREAM, TO SERVE

Melt the butter in a large pan. Add the onion and cook for 5 minutes to soften. Add the garlic, beetroot and potato, cover the pan and sweat for 3 minutes. Pour in the stock and simmer the soup for 1 1/2 hours until the beetroot is tender. Blend until smooth, then sieve. Season if needed. Garnish with parsley and serve with swirls of sour cream. SERVES 6

TOP: Garlic Soup

BOTTOM: Beetroot and Garlic Soup

BOUILLABAISSE

Authentic bouillabaisse uses red gunard, conger eel and rascasse, but a carefully chosen selection of white fish and shellfish will make a good soup. It is accompanied by a spicy, hot condiment called rouille.

Rouille
3 SLICES WHITE BREAD, CRUSTS REMOVED, SOAKED IN MILK
4 cloves GARLIC
5 ml (1 tsp) PAPRIKA
1.25 ml (1/2 tsp) CAYENNE PEPPER
75 ml (5 tbsp) OLIVE OIL

Soup
900 g (2 lb) MIXED WHITE FISH, CLEANED
450 g (1 lb) MIXED SHELLFISH
60 ml (4 tbsp) OLIVE OIL
1 LARGE ONION, CHOPPED
white part of 2 SMALL LEEKS, CHOPPED
4 heads GARLIC, HALVED HORIZONTALLY
1 SMALL BULB FENNEL, SLICED
5 RIPE TOMATOES, SKINNED AND CHOPPED
3 STRIPS ORANGE PEEL
good pinch SAFFRON THREADS
1.5 litre (2 1/2 pints) HOT FISH STOCK (MADE FROM FISH TRIMMINGS)
1 sprig THYME
1 BAY LEAF
CHOPPED PARSLEY, TO GARNISH
slices FRENCH BREAD, TOASTED, TO SERVE

To make the rouille, squeeze the milk from the bread, put in a small blender or food processor with the garlic and spices and work to a thick paste. Gradually add the oil until it has the consistency of thick cream. Set aside. Clean and prepare the fish; remove the skin, and bones and cut into chunks. The shellfish can be left in their shells (remove heads if preferred).

Heat the oil in a very large pan. Add the onion, leeks, garlic and fennel and cook until golden. Add the tomatoes, orange peel, saffron, fish stock and herbs. Bring to the boil and boil until the oil mixes into the stock and does not float. Reduce the heat, add the firm white fish and simmer for 8 minutes. Add the shellfish and delicate white fish and cook for a further 5 minutes. Season if needed. Remove the orange peel and bay leaf. Discard any mussels which have failed to open. Garnish with parsley.

Spread the rouille on toast and place in the bottom of deep bowls, pour in the bouillabaisse, or serve the toast separately to float on top. SERVES 6

RIGHT: Bouillabaisse

Red Pepper and Tomato Soup

450 g (1 lb) RED PEPPERS
30 ml (2 tbsp) OLIVE OIL
1 RED ONION, CHOPPED
3 cloves GARLIC, CRUSHED
450 g (1 lb) RIPE TOMATOES, SKINNED AND CHOPPED
600 ml (1 pint) VEGETABLE STOCK
2.5 ml (1/2 tsp) DRIED BASIL
CHOPPED PARSLEY OR BASIL, TO GARNISH

Grill the peppers under a hot grill, turning them until they are charred on all sides. Place in a plastic bag and set aside for 20 minutes. Heat the oil in a large saucepan, add the onion and garlic and cook gently to soften. Stir in the tomatoes, stock and basil. Simmer for 15 minutes.

Remove the peppers from the bag, peel and discard the skins and seeds. Chop the flesh and add to the pan. Continue to simmer the soup for 15 minutes. Blend until smooth in a blender or food processor. If the soup is too thick, add a little water. Reheat the soup and season to taste. Garnish with chopped parsley or basil.

SERVES 4

Tuscan Bean and Garlic Soup

225 g (8 oz) DRIED CANNELLINI OR OTHER WHITE BEANS, SOAKED OVERNIGHT OR
2 x 440 g (15 1/2 oz) CANS CANNELLINI BEANS, DRAINED
45 ml (3 tbsp) OLIVE OIL
225 g (8 oz) CHOPPED WHITE PART LEEKS
3 large cloves GARLIC, CHOPPED
900 ml (1 1/2 pints) CHICKEN STOCK
30 ml (2 tbsp) CHOPPED PARSLEY

If using dried, soaked beans, drain and rinse in cold water then put in a large saucepan. Add enough water to cover them by at least 7.5 cm (3 inches). Bring to the boil, then simmer for about 1 1/2 hours until tender. Keep them in their liquid until required, then drain.

Heat the oil in a large pan, add the leek and cook for 3-4 minutes longer to soften. Stir in the garlic, cook over a low heat for a further 3-4 minutes but do not allow the garlic to colour. Add the stock and half of the drained cooked or canned beans and simmer for 30 minutes. Purée in a blender or food processor. Return to the pan, add the rest of the beans, season and simmer for 20 minutes. Stir in the parsley. Serve with crusty bread such as ciabatta.

SERVES 4-5

TOP: Red Pepper and Tomato Soup
BOTTOM: Tuscan Bean and Garlic Soup

SALADS

Salads can be a fresh and light accompaniment, or a dish in themselves. For just a hint of garlic, rub the inside of the salad bowl with a cut clove. To increase the flavour, use a garlic dressing and, for real garlic lovers, scatter raw garlic directly onto the salad.

PASTA SALAD WITH BASIL AND GARLIC DRESSING

350 g (12 oz) PASTA SHAPES
2 LARGE RED PEPPERS, ROASTED
(SEE PAGE 28)
55 g (2 oz) PINE NUTS, LIGHTLY TOASTED

Dressing
25 g (1 oz) BASIL LEAVES, WASHED AND DRIED
4 cloves GARLIC
30 ml (2 tbsp) WHITE WINE VINEGAR
5 ml (1 tsp) DIJON MUSTARD
120 ml (8 tbsp) OLIVE OIL

Cook the pasta in a large pan of boiling salted water until *al dente*. Drain, rinse in cold water and drain well. Put in a large bowl. Peel the peppers, discard the seeds and cut into small dice. Add to the pasta with the pine nuts. Chop the basil and garlic using a small blender or food processor. Add the vinegar and mustard, then with the motor running, add the oil. Season with a little salt and pepper. Spoon over the salad and toss. SERVES 6

GREEN SALAD WITH GARLIC DRESSING

2 heads LITTLE GEM LETTUCE
1 head CRISP LETTUCE
1/2 head LOLLO BIANCO
1 bunch WATERCRESS, TRIMMED
1/2 CUCUMBER, SLICED
1 GREEN PEPPER, SEEDED AND SLICED
30 ml (2 tbsp) CHOPPED FRESH HERBS, E.G. CHIVES,
PARSLEY

Dressing
90 ml (6 tbsp) OLIVE OIL
30 ml (2 tbsp) WINE VINEGAR
2 cloves GARLIC, CRUSHED
2.5 ml (1/2 tsp) DIJON MUSTARD
2.5 ml (1/2 tsp) SUGAR
EDIBLE FLOWERS, TO GARNISH

Dry the salad leaves in a spinner, tear into small pieces and put in a large bowl with the watercress, cucumber, pepper and herbs. Put the ingredients for the dressing in a screw-topped jar, season with salt and pepper and shake well until mixed. Pour over the salad. Toss and serve immediately with crusty bread to mop up the garlic dressing. Garnish with edible flowers, e.g. borage, if available. SERVES 4-6

Top: Pasta Salad with Basil and Garlic Dressing
Bottom: Green Salad with Garlic Dressing

RICE, AUBERGINE AND GARLIC SALAD

This salad needs no dressing as the aubergine releases some of the oil that it has been cooked in to moisten the salad.

1 LARGE AUBERGINE

75 ml (5 tbsp) OLIVE OIL

15 cloves GARLIC

175 g (6 oz) LONG GRAIN AND WILD RICE

4 TOMATOES, DICED

1 SMALL RED ONION, FINELY CHOPPED

30 ml (2 tbsp) CHOPPED FRESH PARSLEY

Cut the aubergine into 1.25 cm (^{1}/2 inch) dice, sprinkle with salt and set aside for 30 minutes. Heat 30 ml (2 tbsp) of the oil in a small pan. Add the garlic, cook gently for about 15 minutes until golden and tender. Cool. Cook the rice in boiling salted water until tender. Rinse under cold water, drain and put in a large bowl. Skin and chop the garlic; add to the rice with the tomatoes and onion.

Rinse the aubergine, then dry on kitchen paper. Heat 45 ml (3 tbsp) of the oil with any oil from cooking the garlic in a large frying pan. Add the aubergine and sauté until golden and tender. Cool. Stir into the rice mixture with the parsley.

SERVES 4-6

SWEETCORN AND PEPPER SALAD WITH GARLIC SALSA

A colourful salad with a slightly spicy flavour which makes a good accompaniment to barbecued food.

350 g (12 oz) FROZEN SWEETCORN

1 GREEN PEPPER, SEEDED

1 RED PEPPER, SEEDED

^{1}/2 CUCUMBER, DICED

Salsa

4-5 cloves GARLIC, CHOPPED

30 ml (2 tbsp) RED WINE VINEGAR

1.25 ml (^{1}/2 tsp) CUMIN

1.25 ml (^{1}/2 tsp) DRIED OREGANO

1 GREEN CHILLI, SEEDED AND CHOPPED

75 ml (5 tbsp) OLIVE OIL

5 TOMATOES, SKINNED, SEEDED AND ROUGHLY CHOPPED

small bunch CORIANDER, CHOPPED

Put the sweetcorn in a pan. Cover with water, bring to the boil then simmer for 2-3 minutes. Drain, cool then put in a bowl. Cut the peppers into small dice, add to the sweetcorn with the cucumber.

For the salsa, put the garlic, vinegar, cumin, oregano, chilli and a little salt into a small blender or food processor. Blend until finely chopped. Add the oil and blend to mix. Add the tomatoes but only blend in short bursts, so that they still look partly chopped. Stir into the salad with the coriander.

SERVES 6-8

TOP: Rice, Aubergine and Garlic Salad

BOTTOM: Sweetcorn and Pepper Salad with Garlic Salsa

CALIFORNIAN CHICKEN AND AVOCADO SALAD

4 LARGE, BONELESS CHICKEN BREASTS
15 ml (1 tbsp) OLIVE OIL
5 ml (1 tsp) DRIED OREGANO

Dressing
2 cloves GARLIC, PREFERABLY OAK SMOKED
60 ml (4 tbsp) OLIVE OIL
15 ml (1 tbsp) RED WINE VINEGAR
juice and grated rind 1 SMALL ORANGE

2 LARGE AVOCADOS
3 TOMATOES, DICED
15 ml (1 tbsp) CHOPPED MINT LEAVES OR PARSLEY
SELECTION OF MIXED LETTUCE SUCH AS LOLLO ROSSO, FRISÉE OR OAK LEAF
1 SMALL RED ONION, CUT INTO RINGS, TO GARNISH

Rub the skinless side of the chicken with oil, oregano, salt and pepper. Heat a ridged grill pan or grill and cook the chicken for 15 minutes, turning until cooked through. Cool.

Meanwhile, crush the garlic and mix to a paste with a little olive oil. Whisk in the red wine vinegar, remaining oil, the grated rind of the orange and 45 ml (3 tbsp) of the juice. Season.

Remove the chicken skin, cut into thin strips and mix with the dressing. Halve the avocados and discard the stone. Use a small melon-ball cutter to scoop the flesh into balls. Mix into the chicken with the tomatoes and mint. Toss gently. Arrange the lettuce leaves on plates. Top with the salad and garnish with onion rings.

SERVES 4

POTATO SALAD WITH GARLIC MAYONNAISE

Look out for different varieties of potato, such as La Ratte, Pink Fir Apple or Roseval, which taste good cold.

700 g (1½ lb) SMALL NEW POTATOES OR OTHER VARIETY
60 ml (4 tbsp) MAYONNAISE
45 ml (3 tbsp) PLAIN YOGURT OR SOUR CREAM
15 ml (1 tbsp) WHITE WINE VINEGAR
2 cloves GARLIC, CRUSHED
30 ml (2 tbsp) SNIPPED CHIVES, TO GARNISH

Put the potatoes in a pan of cold water, bring to the boil and simmer for 15-20 minutes or until tender. Drain. Leave very small potatoes whole; large ones can be halved or quartered. For other varieties, peel and cut into large dice. Put potatoes in a large bowl. In a small bowl mix the mayonnaise, yogurt, vinegar and garlic. Season. Fold into the potatoes while they are still warm. Garnish and serve.

For a more substantial salad, add 115 g (4 oz) diced smoked pork sausage, or sliced pepperoni sausage, to the potatoes.

SERVES 4

RIGHT: Californian Chicken and Avocado Salad

SWEET PEPPER SALAD

2 LARGE RED PEPPERS
2 LARGE YELLOW PEPPERS
90 ml (6 tbsp) VIRGIN OLIVE OIL
4 cloves GARLIC, CUT INTO SLIVERS

To Garnish
15 ml (1 tbsp) CHOPPED FLAT-LEAVED PARSLEY
BLACK OLIVES

Pre-heat the grill to high. Grill the peppers, turning them until the skins are black and blistered. Place in a plastic bag, seal and leave to cool for 20 minutes. Peel off the skins, discard stems and seeds. Cut the flesh into strips and arrange in a shallow dish. Drizzle over the olive oil. Scatter over the garlic and marinate for at least 2 hours at room temperature. To store overnight or for up to 3 days, cover with cling film and refrigerate. Garnish with parsley and olives.   SERVES 4-6

SALAD NIÇOISE

This colourful salad makes a lunch dish or first course. Serve with French bread, sun-dried tomato bread or olive bread, if available.

Dressing
2 cloves GARLIC, MASHED
2 ANCHOVY FILLETS
10 ml (2 tsp) BALSAMIC VINEGAR
15 ml (1 tbsp) LEMON JUICE
2.5 ml (½ tsp) DIJON MUSTARD
90 ml (6 tbsp) OLIVE OIL

115 g (4 oz) THIN GREEN BEANS, COOKED AND COOLED
225 g (8 oz) BABY NEW POTATOES, COOKED
AND COOLED
6 SPRING ONIONS, CHOPPED
175 g (6 oz) CHERRY TOMATOES, HALVED, IF WISHED
1 x 200 g (7 oz) CAN TUNA, DRAINED AND FLAKED
85 g (3 oz) BLACK OLIVES, STONED
1 CRISP LETTUCE, WASHED AND DRIED
3 HARD-BOILED EGGS
1 x 55 g (2 oz) CAN ANCHOVIES, DRAINED

To make the dressing, purée the garlic, the anchovies (taken from the can listed with the other ingredients), vinegar, lemon juice and mustard in a blender or food processor. With the motor still running, add the oil.

Cut the beans into short lengths and halve or quarter the potatoes. In a large bowl combine all the salad ingredients except the eggs and anchovies. Add the dressing and toss. Arrange the lettuce on a platter and spoon over the salad. Quarter the eggs and arrange on the salad. Halve the anchovy fillets lengthwise and arrange in criss-cross on top.   SERVES 4

TOP: Sweet Pepper Salad
BOTTOM: Salad Niçoise

SUMMER SALAD WITH GARLIC CROÛTONS

1 large clove GARLIC, HALVED
2 handfuls CURLY ENDIVE (FRISÉE)
1 head LETTUCE, E.G. LOLLO BIONDO, CRISP
GREEN LETTUCE, WASHED AND DRIED
1 RED PEPPER, SEEDED AND DICED
1/2 CUCUMBER, PEELED AND DICED
1 head FENNEL, SLICED
1/2 bunch SPRING ONIONS, TRIMMED AND CHOPPED
3 TOMATOES, CUT INTO STRIPS

Dressing
45 ml (3 tbsp) SUNFLOWER OIL
15 ml (1 tbsp) OLIVE OIL
15 ml (1 tbsp) RED WINE VINEGAR
2.5 ml (1/2 tsp) DIJON MUSTARD

Croûtons
2 LARGE THICK SLICES BREAD
OIL FOR FRYING
3 cloves GARLIC, VERY FINELY CHOPPED

Rub the inside of the salad bowl with the halved clove of garlic. Prepare the salad ingredients and put in the bowl. Mix the dressing. Remove the crusts from the bread and cut into small cubes. Heat enough oil in a pan to deep-fry the croûtons, add the cubed bread and fry until golden and crisp. Remove with a slotted spoon and drain on kitchen paper.

Mix the garlic and 2.5 ml (1/2 tsp) salt together, put in a bowl, add the croûtons and toss. Cool. Add the dressing to the salad and toss. Scatter over the croûtons. For an extra garlicky salad scatter the chopped garlic.

SERVES 4-6

BEAN AND GARLIC SALAD

Borlotti beans look attractive with the green beans but use other varieties if preferred. If using dried beans, soak them the day before preparing the salad.

225 g (8 oz) DRIED BORLOTTI BEANS,
SOAKED OVERNIGHT OR
2 x 440 g (15 1/2 oz) CANS BORLOTTI BEANS, DRAINED
225 g (8 oz) RUNNER BEANS

Dressing
60 ml (4 tbsp) OLIVE OIL
4-5 cloves GARLIC, FINELY CHOPPED
15 ml (1 tbsp) RED WINE VINEGAR
30 ml (2 tbsp) CHOPPED PARSLEY

Drain the borlotti beans, cover with water and bring to the boil. Simmer until almost tender (about 1 hour). Add salt to taste and cook slowly until tender.

Meanwhile, trim the runner beans and slice diagonally in thin strips. Cook in a little boiling salted water for 3-4 minutes. Drain both pans and put beans in a bowl. Heat the oil in a small pan, add the garlic and cook until golden. Remove from the heat, swirl in the vinegar, pour over the beans and toss. Scatter over the parsley. Cool.

SERVES 6-8

RIGHT: Summer Salad with Garlic Croûtons

CHINESE CHICKEN SALAD

4 BONELESS SKINLESS CHICKEN BREASTS
2.5 cm (1 inch) FRESH GINGER, CUT INTO STRIPS
2 cloves GARLIC, HALVED

Dressing
15 ml (1 tbsp) SESAME OIL
30 ml (2 tbsp) SUNFLOWER OIL
15 ml (1 tbsp) LIGHT SOY SAUCE
15 ml (1 tbsp) RICE WINE, VINEGAR OR CIDER VINEGAR
2-3 cloves GARLIC, CRUSHED
5 ml (1 tsp) CHILLI SAUCE

Salad
115 g (4 oz) BEANSPROUTS, WASHED AND TRIMMED
115 g (4 oz) BUTTON MUSHROOMS, SLICED
5 SPRING ONIONS, CHOPPED
10 cm (4 inch) piece CUCUMBER, SLICED OR DICED
1 GREEN PEPPER, SEEDED AND CUT INTO THIN STRIPS
TOASTED OR BLACK SESAME SEEDS, TO GARNISH

Put the chicken in a pan, add water to just cover. Add the ginger and garlic and simmer for about 10 minutes until the chicken is cooked. Leave to cool in the liquid.

Cube the chicken and transfer to a large serving bowl. Mix the ingredients for the dressing, pour over the chicken. Add the ingredients for the salad to the chicken and toss. Sprinkle with sesame seeds.　SERVES 4

WARM LENTIL SALAD

Puy lentils have a distinctive flavour, they are slate green in colour and hold their shape during cooking. Serve warm with grilled meats.

225 g (8 oz) PUY LENTILS
2 BAY LEAVES
2 sprigs THYME
45 ml (3 tbsp) OLIVE OIL
1 MEDIUM RED ONION, FINELY CHOPPED
1 LARGE CARROT, FINELY DICED
2 sticks CELERY, FINELY DICED
3 cloves GARLIC, THINLY SLICED
30 ml (2 tbsp) BALSAMIC OR RED WINE VINEGAR
45 ml (3 tbsp) CHOPPED PARSLEY

Rinse the lentils then put in a large saucepan with bay leaves and thyme and cover with cold water. Bring to the boil, then simmer gently for 15 minutes. Add salt to taste and simmer a further 5-10 minutes until tender.

While the lentils are simmering, heat the oil in a large frying pan. Add the onion, carrot and celery and cook gently for about 8 minutes until they begin to soften. Add the garlic and cook a further 2 minutes. Drain the lentils, discard the herbs and stir the lentils into the vegetables with the vinegar and parsley.　SERVES 4

RIGHT: Chinese Chicken Salad

FISH DISHES

Many of these fish and seafood recipes have a strong Mediterranean flavour. They are inspired by the tastes and aromas of the cooking of these warm countries. All the ingredients are available from supermarkets or fishmongers.

SEAFOOD PAELLA

45 ml (3 tbsp) OLIVE OIL

250 g (9 oz) MONKFISH FILLET, SKINNED, CUT INTO BITE-SIZED CHUNKS

1 MEDIUM SPANISH ONION, CHOPPED

5 cloves GARLIC, THINLY SLICED

1 RED PEPPER, SEEDED AND CHOPPED

250 g (9 oz) RISOTTO RICE

700 ml (1¼ pint) FISH STOCK

150 ml (5 fl oz) DRY WHITE WINE

few SAFFRON THREADS

400 g (14 oz) PREPARED MIXED SHELLFISH, E.G. COOKED MUSSELS, SQUID, PRAWNS, SCALLOPS THAWED IF FROZEN (THIS MIXTURE CAN OFTEN BE PURCHASED FROZEN)

115 g (4 oz) FROZEN PEAS

To Garnish

sprigs PARSLEY

LEMON WEDGES

Heat the oil in a paella pan or large shallow casserole. Add the monkfish and fry over a moderate heat for 5 minutes. Remove with a slotted spoon and set aside. Add the onion, increase the heat and fry until soft. Stir in the garlic and pepper and cook for 2 minutes. Add the rice and stir until it is coated with the onion mixture. Pour in the stock and wine, add the saffron and bring to the boil. Simmer uncovered for 20 minutes.

Add the monkfish and continue to cook for 5-10 minutes until most of the stock has been absorbed and the rice is tender. Stir the prepared shellfish into the rice with the peas and cook for 5 minutes for the shellfish to reheat. Add a little more stock if necessary. Season and garnish with parsley and lemon wedges.   SERVES 4

RIGHT: Seafood Paella

MEDITERRANEAN FISH STEW

᪥

60 ml (4 tbsp) OLIVE OIL

350 g (12 oz) POTATOES, PEELED AND DICED

1 SMALL ONION, FINELY CHOPPED

1 RED PEPPER, SEEDED AND SLICED

4 cloves GARLIC, THINLY SLICED

5 ml (1 tsp) PAPRIKA

450 g (1 lb) PLUM TOMATOES, SKINNED AND CHOPPED

120 ml (8 fl oz) DRY WHITE WINE

450 g (1 lb) COD FILLET, SKINNED

175 g (6 oz) FROZEN, PEELED PRAWNS

CHOPPED PARSLEY, TO GARNISH

Heat the oil in a large saucepan or deep frying pan. Add the potatoes, onion and red pepper and cook gently for 10 minutes, stirring constantly. Add the garlic and paprika and cook for a further minute. Stir in the tomatoes, wine and 150 ml (1/4 pint) water and simmer, uncovered, for about 25 minutes until the potato is just tender.

Cut the fish into large chunks, add to the pan with the prawns and cook gently for about 5-8 minutes until the fish begins to flake. Garnish with the parsley and serve.

SERVES 4

SAUTÉED MONKFISH WITH NIÇOISE SAUCE

᪥

The very highly flavoured sauce complements the firm texture of the fish. This recipe also works well with swordfish or tuna steaks.

55 g (2 oz) BLACK OLIVES, PITTED

20 ml (4 tsp) SUN-DRIED TOMATO PASTE OR 3-4 SUN-DRIED TOMATOES

10 ml (2 tsp) CAPERS, DRAINED

1-2 ANCHOVY FILLETS

55 g (2 oz) BUTTER

4 cloves GARLIC, CRUSHED

450 g (1 lb) MONKFISH FILLETS, SKINNED, CUT INTO 1.25 CM (1/2 INCH) SLICES

30 ml (2 tbsp) CHOPPED PARSLEY, TO GARNISH

Put the olives, sun-dried tomato paste, capers and anchovies in a small blender or food processor to finely chop. Heat the butter in a frying pan, add the garlic and cook gently for 1-2 minutes – do not brown. Add the fish and sauté for about 5-7 minutes until just cooked. Add the niçoise sauce, and continue to cook for 3-4 minutes, turning the pieces of fish to coat with sauce. Garnish and serve immediately.

SERVES 4

TOP: Mediterranean Fish Stew

BOTTOM: Sautéed Monkfish with Niçoise Sauce

MOULES MARINIÈRE

1.8 kg (4 lb) MUSSELS
2-3 SHALLOTS, FINELY CHOPPED
3 cloves GARLIC, FINELY CHOPPED
30 ml (2 tbsp) CHOPPED PARSLEY
210 ml (7 fl oz) DRY WHITE WINE
25 g (1 oz) BUTTER
15 g (½ oz) FLOUR
EXTRA PARSLEY, TO GARNISH

Scrape, scrub and thoroughly clean the mussels under running water. Pull away the beard and throw away any that are cracked, or that remain open when tapped. Put the shallots, garlic, parsley and wine into the largest pan possible and simmer for 10 minutes. Add the mussels, put the lid on and cook over a high heat for about 5 minutes. Shake the pan once or twice during cooking.

Mash the butter and flour together. Pour off the cooking juices into another saucepan and boil for 3 minutes. Remove from the heat, whisk in the butter and flour paste, return to the heat and bring to the boil. Season, if needed, with pepper. Lift the mussels into deep soup plates, discarding any that have not opened. Pour over the sauce and sprinkle with parsley. Serve with crusty French bread.

SERVES 4 AS A STARTER OR 2 AS A MAIN COURSE

SCALLOPS PROVENÇAL

Use queen scallops for this dish; they are small in size and have a wonderful flavour. Alternatively, use the larger size and cut them in half.

500 g (1¼ lb) QUEEN SCALLOPS
30 ml (2 tbsp) OLIVE OIL
1 MEDIUM ONION, FINELY CHOPPED
4 cloves GARLIC, THINLY SLICED
450 g (1 lb) RIPE TOMATOES, SKINNED AND CHOPPED
5 ml (1 tsp) TOMATO PURÉE
5 ml (1 tsp) FRESH THYME
150 ml (5 fl oz) DRY WHITE WINE
30 ml (2 tbsp) CHOPPED PARSLEY, TO GARNISH

Wash the scallops, leave the corals attached, then drain in a colander and trim off any black veins. Heat the oil in a frying pan and gently cook the onion until softened. Add the garlic and after a few seconds stir in the tomatoes, tomato purée, thyme and wine. Simmer, uncovered, for 15-20 minutes until the sauce becomes pulpy. Season. Stir in the scallops and cook for 3 minutes (any longer and they will become tough). Garnish and serve immediately.

SERVES 4

Top: Scallops Provençal
Bottom: Moules Marinière

TROUT IN LEMON GARLIC SAUCE

Try this recipe with other small whole fish such as talapia or small red snapper.

4 TROUT, CLEANED
30 ml (2 tbsp) LEMON JUICE
rind of 1 LEMON, COARSELY GRATED
25 g (1 oz) BUTTER
20 cloves GARLIC, PEELED
300 ml (½ pint) SINGLE CREAM

Pre-heat the oven to 190°C (375°F/Gas mark 5). Slash the trout 2 or 3 times on each side, then place in a shallow ovenproof dish. Pour over the lemon juice, add the rind, dot with butter and tuck the cloves of garlic in amongst the fish. Cover with foil. Bake for about 25 minutes until the fish is tender.

Meanwhile, pour the cream into a small pan, simmer until thick and reduced by about half. Set aside. Pour off the juices from the fish. Remove the garlic. Press through a sieve and blend the purée back into the juices. Stir the mixture into the cream, reheat gently; do not boil. Serve the trout with the sauce. SERVES 4

PLAICE WITH LEEK AND GARLIC STUFFING

6 LARGE PLAICE FILLETS, SKINNED

Stuffing
225 g (8 oz) LEEKS, TRIMMED (LEAVE SOME OF THE GREEN PART)
25 g (1 oz) BUTTER
3 cloves GARLIC, FINELY CHOPPED OR CRUSHED
25 g (1 oz) GROUND ALMONDS
20 g (¾ oz) BUTTER
45 g (1½ oz) FRESH BROWN BREADCRUMBS
25 g (1 oz) FLAKED ALMONDS
30 ml (2 tbsp) CHOPPED PARSLEY

Pre-heat the oven to 190°C (375°F/Gas mark 5). Skin the fillets and divide each one along the central line into 2 fillets. Quarter the leeks lengthways, wash and drain, then thinly slice. Melt the butter in a small pan, add the leeks and garlic, stir well and cook gently until the leeks are tender. Remove from the heat, stir in the ground almonds and season. Cool. Put a spoonful of the stuffing at the thick end of each plaice fillet, roll up and put in a buttered ovenproof dish. Cover with foil and bake for 20 minutes.

Meanwhile melt the butter in a frying pan, add the breadcrumbs and cook, stirring, until they start to crisp. Add the almonds and cook for 1-2 minutes until golden. Remove from the heat, add the parsley. Remove the fish from the oven. Transfer to serving plates, spoon over a little juice and top with the golden crumbs. SERVES 4

TOP: Trout in Lemon Garlic Sauce
BOTTOM: Plaice with Leek and Garlic Stuffing

HADDOCK WITH LIME AND CORIANDER

☙

15 ml (1 tbsp) SUNFLOWER OIL
8 SPRING ONIONS, FINELY CHOPPED
4 cloves GARLIC, FINELY CHOPPED
30 ml (2 tbsp) CHOPPED CORIANDER LEAVES
grated rind and juice 2 LIMES
4 THICK HADDOCK FILLETS, SKINNED

To Garnish
1 LIME, CUT INTO WEDGES
CORIANDER LEAVES

Pre-heat the oven to 190°C (375°F/Gas mark 5). Heat the oil in a small pan, add the spring onions and garlic and cook for 1 minute. Remove from the heat, add the coriander, lime rind and juice. Season.

Put the haddock fillets in an ovenproof dish, spoon over the topping, cover and bake for 20 minutes until the fish is cooked. Garnish with lime wedges and coriander leaves.

SERVES 4

KING PRAWNS WITH GARLIC AND GINGER

☙

Raw tiger prawns are now more readily available at fish counters in supermarkets, alternatively buy ready cooked king prawns.

450 g (1 lb) LARGE, UNCOOKED PEELED TIGER
PRAWN TAILS
30 ml (2 tbsp) VEGETABLE OIL
4 cloves GARLIC, FINELY CHOPPED
4 cm (1½ inches) FRESH GINGER, FINELY CHOPPED
grated rind of 1 LIME
10 ml (2 tsp) FISH SAUCE OR LIGHT SOY SAUCE
4 SPRING ONIONS, THINLY SLICED

Rinse and dry the prawns on kitchen paper. Use a frying pan large enough to take the prawns in a single layer. Heat the oil, add the garlic and ginger and gently cook for 1 minute. Turn up the heat and add the prawns. Turn them in the pan and fry them long enough to cook the flesh (when they will turn pink – about 2 minutes). Stir in the lime rind and fish sauce and 30 ml (2 tbsp) water. Simmer for 1 minute. Stir in the spring onions. Serve immediately.

SERVES 4

TOP: *Haddock with Lime and Coriander*
BOTTOM: *King Prawns with Garlic and Ginger*

MEAT AND POULTRY

Garlic can be added in abundance to many meat dishes to achieve rich, strong flavours which will satisfy the healthiest of appetites. Try gremolata with turkey steaks on casseroles or braises or try adding a little raw garlic to a cooked dish as a final flourish.

CHICKEN WITH 50 CLOVES OF GARLIC

The garlic imparts a delicious aroma to the chicken – even more than 50 cloves can be used. The cooked cloves taste mild and nutty; they can be squeezed from their skins and eaten with accompanying vegetables.

1.5 kg (3-3 1/2 lb) CHICKEN, PREFERABLY CORN-FED
1/2 LEMON
sprigs THYME OR ROSEMARY
50 cloves GARLIC, UNPEELED
60 ml (4 tbsp) OLIVE OIL
30 ml (2 tbsp) PLAIN FLOUR

Pre-heat the oven to 190°C (375°F/Gas mark 5). Stuff the chicken with the lemon and some thyme. Place in an earthenware casserole, or ovenproof dish with a lid. Remove the papery outer skins from the garlic. Add to the dish, then pour over the oil making sure the chicken and garlic are coated. Scatter over some more herbs and season.

Mix the flour with enough water to form a dough; roll into a thin roll. Moisten the rim of the cooking pot with water, then press the dough onto the edge. Put on the lid and the dough will create a seal. Cook in the oven for 1 1/2 hours. Serve the chicken with the cloves of garlic.

SERVES 4

GREEK LAMB AND PASTA BAKE

Orzo is pasta shaped like grains of rice, available from Italian food stores. The garlic melts into the pasta during cooking, giving the dish a rich, satisfying taste. The dish is ready when the pasta is tender.

8 SMALL LEAN LAMB CHUMP CHOPS
4 LARGE CLOVES GARLIC, HALVED
OR QUARTERED
600 ml (1 pint) STOCK
1 x 400 g (14 oz) CAN CHOPPED TOMATOES
45 ml (3 tbsp) EXTRA VIRGIN OLIVE OIL
10 ml (2 tsp) DRIED OREGANO
225 g (8 oz) ORZO

Pre-heat the oven to 200°C (400°F/Gas mark 6). Place the chops in a large ovenproof dish, so they lie in a single layer. Scatter over the pieces of garlic, pour over half the stock, the tomatoes, oil and oregano. Season to taste, cover and place in the oven. Cook for 45 minutes. Remove from the oven, pour over the remaining stock and stir in the orzo; ensure it is covered in liquid. Return to the oven for 40 minutes. Stir once or twice while cooking.

SERVES 4

RIGHT: Chicken with 50 Cloves of Garlic

GARLIC ROAST PORK

If the crumb crust falls off during carving, spoon onto the slices of roast pork to serve.

1.35 kg (3 lb) BONED PORK LOIN
6 large cloves GARLIC, FINELY CHOPPED
45 ml (3 tbsp) CHOPPED PARSLEY
5 ml (1 tsp) CHOPPED ROSEMARY SPRIGS
55 g (2 oz) HAM, FINELY CHOPPED
45 ml (3 tbsp) OLIVE OIL
150 ml (5 fl oz) DRY WHITE WINE
450 ml (3/4 pint) CHICKEN STOCK
55 g (2 oz) FRESH WHITE BREADCRUMBS
15 ml (1 tbsp) CORNFLOUR

Trim off the rind and as much fat as possible from the pork. Pre-heat the oven to 200°C (400°F/Gas mark 6). Mix the garlic, parsley and rosemary together. Season with salt and pepper. Mix half this mixture with the ham.

Open out the pork and spread the ham mixture over it. Roll up and tie with string. Brush the joint with 15 ml (1 tbsp) of the oil. Place in a roasting dish, underside up. Cook for 30 minutes. Turn the joint over and add the wine and 150 ml (1/4 pint) of the stock. Baste the meat. Cook for a further 30 minutes.

Meanwhile, mix the remaining garlic mixture with the breadcrumbs and remaining oil. Remove the joint from the oven, cut off the strings and press the crumb mixture over the pork. Lower the oven temperature to 180°C (350°F/Gas mark 4) and cook for 40 minutes until the crust is golden and crisp. Transfer the joint to a carving board. Pour the remaining stock in a dish and scrape up any brown pieces of meat; pour into a pan. Blend the cornflour with 45 ml (3 tbsp) water, add to pan and simmer the gravy to thicken. Strain into a serving jug. Carve the pork and serve with the gravy.   SERVES 4-6

SPICY COCONUT CHICKEN CURRY

1 MEDIUM ONION, ROUGHLY CHOPPED
5 large cloves GARLIC, ROUGHLY CHOPPED
2 stalks LEMON GRASS
1-2 SMALL RED CHILLIES, SEEDED AND ROUGHLY CHOPPED
5 cm (2 inch) PIECE FRESH GINGER, PEELED AND CHOPPED
10 ml (2 tsp) PAPRIKA
2.5 ml (1/2 tsp) CORIANDER
5 ml (1 tsp) CUMIN
1.25 ml (1/4 tsp) TURMERIC
30 ml (2 tbsp) VEGETABLE OIL
8 CHICKEN THIGHS, SKINNED AND BONED
1 x 400 g (14 oz) CAN COCONUT MILK
small bunch CORIANDER, TO GARNISH

Put the onion, garlic, the bottom 10 cm (4 inches) of the lemon grass stem, chillies and ginger in a blender or food processor. Add the spices and blend to a paste. In a large frying pan, heat the oil and cook the paste for 4-5 minutes. Cut the chicken thighs into chunks, add to the pan and turn in the mixture to coat. Add the coconut milk and simmer uncovered for 25-30 minutes until the chicken is tender, stirring occasionally. Shred the coriander leaves and garnish. Serve with rice.   SERVES 4

RIGHT: Garlic Roast Pork

STEAK PIZZAIOLA

45 ml (3 tbsp) OLIVE OIL

1 SMALL ONION, THINLY SLICED

4 cloves GARLIC, SLICED

1 x 400 g (14 oz) CAN CHOPPED TOMATOES

5 ml (1 tsp) DICED OREGANO OR BASIL

4 x 200 g (7 oz) SIRLOIN STEAKS

30 ml (1 fl oz) DRY WHITE WINE

8 BLACK OLIVES, PITTED AND SLICED (OPTIONAL)

Heat 30 ml (2 tbsp) of the oil in a sauté pan. Add the onion and cook for 3-4 minutes. Add the garlic and when it begins to turn golden add the tomatoes, oregano or basil. Simmer for about 12-15 minutes. Season with salt and pepper.

Heat a large heavy-based frying pan. Add the remaining oil, then the steaks, and cook on both sides just enough to brown them. Pour over the wine, then the tomato sauce. Turn the steaks in the sauce, then cover the pan and simmer for 5 minutes. Serve the steaks, each topped with the sauce and olives, if using.

SERVES 4

TURKEY STEAKS MILANESE

Top the steaks with an aromatic mixture called gremolata just before serving, so that the aroma of the citrus peel is retained.

15 g (1/2 oz) BUTTER

30 ml (2 tbsp) OLIVE OIL

4 TURKEY BREAST STEAKS

4 cloves GARLIC, HALVED

150 ml (5 fl oz) DRY WHITE WINE

300 ml (1/2 pint) WELL-FLAVOURED TURKEY OR CHICKEN STOCK

2 sprigs FRESH ROSEMARY OR

5 ml (1 tsp) DRIED ROSEMARY

Gremolata

30 ml (2 tbsp) CHOPPED PARSLEY

grated rind 1 LEMON

1 clove GARLIC, FINELY CHOPPED

5 ml (1 tsp) CORNFLOUR

75 ml (5 tbsp) SINGLE CREAM

Heat the butter and oil in a large frying pan so the steaks can cook in a single layer. Add the steaks and lightly brown on both sides. Add the garlic and when pale golden, pour off the excess fat. Add the wine and stock. Break the sprig of rosemary into 2 or 3 pieces and add to the pan. Cover and simmer for 15-20 minutes until the turkey is tender.

For the gremolata, combine the parsley, lemon rind and chopped garlic. Set aside. Transfer the turkey to a serving dish. Keep warm. Remove the garlic and rosemary from the pan and discard. Blend the cornflour with the cream and stir into the sauce. Simmer to thicken, season to taste. Pour the sauce over the steaks and scatter over the gremolata.

SERVES 4

TOP: Steak Pizzaiola

BOTTOM: Turkey Steaks Milanese

MOROCCAN CHICKEN CASSEROLE

1.5 kg (3¹/2 lb) CHICKEN CUT INTO 8 PIECES
60 ml (4 tbsp) LEMON JUICE
45 ml (3 tbsp) VIRGIN OLIVE OIL
15 ml (1 tbsp) FINELY CHOPPED GARLIC
5 ml (1 tsp) GROUND GINGER
5 ml (1 tsp) CUMIN
5 ml (1 tsp) GROUND CORIANDER
5 ml (1 tsp) CINNAMON
large pinch SAFFRON THREADS
2.5 ml (¹/2 tsp) GROUND BLACK PEPPER
1 MEDIUM ONION, THINLY SLICED
600 ml (1 pint) CHICKEN STOCK
175 g (6 oz) READY-TO-EAT PRUNES, PITTED
10 ml (2 tsp) CORNFLOUR
small bunch CORIANDER LEAVES

Put the chicken pieces in a large ovenproof dish, pour over the lemon juice and oil, then scatter over the garlic. Marinate for 2-4 hours.

Pre-heat oven to 180°C (350°F/Gas mark 4). Mix the spices together, sprinkle over the chicken, add the onion and stock then cover and cook in the oven for 1 hour.

Stir in the prunes and cook for a further 30 minutes. Blend the cornflour with a little water and stir into the casserole. Add salt, if needed, and return to the oven for 15 minutes until the sauce has thickened. Shred the coriander leaves and scatter over the casserole. Serve with steamed couscous.   SERVES 4

LAMB KOFTA WITH ONION AND GARLIC RELISH

Kofta
700 g (1¹/2 lb) MINCED LAMB
1 MEDIUM ONION, GRATED
2 cloves GARLIC, FINELY CHOPPED
30 ml (2 tbsp) CHOPPED PARSLEY
15 ml (1 tbsp) CHOPPED CORIANDER LEAVES
10 ml (2 tsp) GROUND CORIANDER
5 ml (1 tsp) CUMIN
2.5 ml (¹/2 tsp) CINNAMON

Relish
60 ml (4 tbsp) OLIVE OIL
450 g (1 lb) ONIONS, THINLY SLICED
15 ml (1 tbsp) SUGAR
15 ml (1 tbsp) FINELY CHOPPED GARLIC
30 ml (2 tbsp) WHITE WINE VINEGAR

Put all the ingredients for the kofta into a bowl. Season to taste. Knead the mixture by hand until it looks paste-like. Cover and refrigerate for 2 hours.

Meanwhile, make the relish. Heat the oil in a heavy-based frying pan. Add the onions and sugar and cook until softened and golden. Stir in the garlic and cook for 1 minute. Add the vinegar and continue to cook until almost all of the liquid has evaporated and the onions are tender. Season. Set aside.

Divide the lamb mixture into 16 portions, roll each portion into a sausage shape. Place on a grill pan and cook under a medium hot grill, for about 15 minutes, turning the koftas until browned all over. Serve with the warm relish and a salad.   SERVES 4

TOP: *Moroccan Chicken Casserole*
BOTTOM: *Lamb Kofta with Onion and Garlic Relish*

ORIENTAL CHICKEN WITH NOODLES

700 g (1½ lb) SKINLESS, BONELESS CHICKEN BREAST
60 ml (4 tbsp) LIME JUICE
45 ml (3 tbsp) SOY SAUCE
4 cloves GARLIC, FINELY CHOPPED
2 RED CHILLIES, SEEDED AND FINELY CHOPPED
5 ml (1 tsp) SUGAR
115 g (4 oz) THREAD EGG NOODLES
30 ml (2 tbsp) VEGETABLE OIL
4 SPRING ONIONS, TRIMMED AND CHOPPED, OR MADE INTO TASSLES, TO GARNISH

Chop the chicken into very small pieces. Put in a bowl with the lime juice, soy sauce, garlic, chillies and sugar. Stir, cover and set aside for 1 hour. Bring a large pan of water to the boil, add the noodles, cover, then turn off the heat.

Heat the oil in a large frying pan or wok. Add the chicken mixture and cook, stirring constantly for 5-6 minutes. Drain the noodles, stir into the chicken mixture and mix for 1 minute. Garnish and serve immediately.

SERVES 4

BEEF AND PEPPER STIR FRY

225 g (8 oz) BROCCOLI
15 ml (1 tbsp) SESAME OIL
15 ml (1 tbsp) SUNFLOWER OIL
450 g (1 lb) RUMP STEAK, CUT INTO THIN STRIPS
1 RED PEPPER, SEEDED AND THINLY SLICED
1 YELLOW PEPPER, SEEDED AND THINLY SLICED
5 SPRING ONIONS, SLICED DIAGONALLY
15 ml (1 tbsp) CHOPPED FRESH GINGER
3 cloves GARLIC, THINLY SLICED
30 ml (2 tbsp) DRY SHERRY
1.25 ml (¼ tsp) CHINESE FIVE SPICE POWDER
30 ml (2 tbsp) DARK SOY SAUCE
5 ml (1 tsp) CORNFLOUR
SESAME SEEDS (OPTIONAL)

Divide the broccoli into small florets and thinly slice the stalks. Heat both oils in a wok or large sauté pan. Add the beef and brown for 2-3 minutes. Remove with a slotted spoon.

Add the vegetables to the pan with the ginger and garlic and stir-fry for 3-4 minutes. Stir in the sherry, spice powder and soy sauce, then return the beef to the pan. Blend the cornflour with 45 ml (3 tbsp) water, add to the pan and simmer until the sauce thickens. Transfer to a dish, sprinkle with sesame seeds, if wished, and serve with rice or noodles.

SERVES 4

TOP: *Oriental Chicken with Noodles*
BOTTOM: *Beef and Pepper Stir Fry*

CASSOULET DE PROVENCE

❧

For a variation, omit half of the fresh sausages and add 227 g (8 oz) smoked pork sausage cut into thick slices. Haricot beans are traditionally used in cassoulet, but borlotti and red kidney beans taste good too.

350 g (12 oz) PORK STREAKY RASHERS, RINDS REMOVED
225 g (8 oz) PIECE SMOKED BACON
60 ml (4 tbsp) OLIVE OIL
450 g (1 lb) COARSE PORK SAUSAGES
1 LARGE SPANISH ONION, CHOPPED
2.5 ml (1/2 tsp) CHILLI POWDER
12 cloves GARLIC
1 x 400 g (14 oz) CAN CHOPPED TOMATOES
15 ml (1 tbsp) TOMATO PURÉE
150 ml (5 fl oz) DRY WHITE WINE
450 ml (3/4 pint) STOCK
bunch FRESH HERBS
1 x 425 g (15 oz) CAN HARICOT BEANS, DRAINED
1 x 440 g (15 1/2 oz) CAN LIMA OR BROAD BEANS, DRAINED
1 x 200 g (7 oz) SMALL CRUSTY WHITE BATON OR FRENCH STICK

Pre-heat the oven to 170°C (325°F/Gas mark 3). Cut the pork and bacon into bite-sized pieces. Heat half the oil in a large flame-proof casserole, add the pork, bacon and sausages and cook until lightly browned. Remove from the pan, cut the sausages into 3 and set aside. Stir the onion into the casserole and cook until golden. Mix in the chilli powder and garlic and cook for 1 minute. Stir in the tomatoes, tomato purée, wine, stock, herbs and beans. Return the meats to the casserole (and sliced smoked pork sausage, if using). Bring the liquid to the boil, then cover and bake for 1 1/4 hours.

Meanwhile, make rough breadcrumbs from the French bread and toss them in the remaining oil. Increase the oven temperature to 190°C (375°F/Gas mark 5). Remove the herbs from the casserole and sprinkle over the breadcrumbs. Return, uncovered, to the oven for 30 minutes or until golden.   SERVES 6

PORK CHOPS WITH GARLIC PEARLS AND MUSTARD SAUCE

❧

4 x 175 g (6 oz) BONELESS LOIN PORK CHOPS
15 ml (1 tbsp) DIJON MUSTARD
24 cloves GARLIC, PEELED
150 ml (5 fl oz) DRY WHITE WINE
450 ml (3/4 pint) CHICKEN STOCK
10 ml (2 tsp) CORNFLOUR
60 ml (4 tbsp) SINGLE CREAM
5 ml (1 tsp) WHOLE GRAIN MUSTARD

Pre-heat the oven to 180°C (350°F/Gas mark 4). Season the chops, spread the mustard over them, then place in an ovenproof dish. Arrange the garlic cloves around the chops. Pour over the wine and stock, cover and cook for 1 1/4 hours until the pork is tender. Transfer the chops to a warmed serving dish. Keep warm. Strain the cooking juices into a pan, reserving the garlic, and boil for 5 minutes. Blend the cornflour with the cream, stir into the pan with the mustard and simmer to thicken. To serve, place a chop on each plate, pour over the sauce, garnish with the garlic cloves.   SERVES 4

TOP: Cassoulet de Provence

BOTTOM: Pork Chops with Garlic Pearls and Mustard Sauce

ROAST LAMB WITH GARLIC AND ROSEMARY

The flavour of oak-smoked garlic is slightly milder than fresh garlic.

1.5 kg (3½ lb) LEG OF LAMB
16 small sprigs ROSEMARY
1-2 cloves GARLIC, CUT INTO 16 SLIVERS
15 ml (1 tbsp) OLIVE OIL
1 head GARLIC OR OAK-SMOKED GARLIC
150 ml (5 fl oz) RED WINE
15 ml (1 tbsp) PLAIN FLOUR
600 ml (1 pint) LAMB STOCK

Pre-heat the oven to 200°C (400°F/Gas Mark 6). Use the point of a sharp knife to make 16 slits all over the lamb and insert the sprigs of rosemary and slivers of garlic. Place in a roasting tin and brush over the olive oil. Season. Separate the head of garlic into cloves. Peel, then tuck the cloves under the lamb. Roast for 30 minutes. Reduce the oven temperature to 180°C (350°F/Gas mark 4). Pour over the red wine and cook for a further 1 hour, basting 2-3 times during cooking.

Transfer the lamb to a serving dish, cover and keep warm. Skim off the fat from the pan juices, crush the garlic and mash into the juices. Add the flour and cook for 1 minute on the stove. Add the stock, bring to the boil and simmer for 5 minutes. Season, then strain into a gravy boat.   SERVES 6

SPANISH CHICKEN CASSEROLE

45 ml (3 tbsp) OLIVE OIL
1.5 kg (3½ lb) CHICKEN CUT INTO 8 PIECES
1 SPANISH ONION, CHOPPED
2 RED PEPPERS, SEEDED, CUT INTO 1.25 CM (½ INCH) STRIPS
5 cloves GARLIC, ROUGHLY CRUSHED
85 g (3 oz) HAM, DICED
1 x 400 g (14 oz) CAN CHOPPED TOMATOES
180 ml (6 fl oz) MEDIUM (OLOROSO) SHERRY
1 BAY LEAF
5 ml (1 tsp) DRIED MEDITERRANEAN HERBS
55 g (2 oz) BLACK OR GREEN OLIVES, PITTED

Heat the oil in a large shallow casserole, add the chicken pieces and cook until golden brown. Remove from the pan and set aside. Add the onion and cook for 5 minutes until golden. Add the peppers and stir until slightly softened. Stir in the garlic and ham and sauté for 1 minute. Stir in the tomatoes and sherry, add the bay leaf, herbs and olives and simmer. Return the chicken to the casserole, cover and simmer for 1½ hours.

Season and discard the bay leaf. If wished, the sauce can be thickened with 10 ml (2 tsp) cornflour blended with a little water. Serve with rice or potatoes.   SERVES 4

TOP: Roast Lamb with Garlic and Rosemary
BOTTOM: Spanish Chicken Casserole

SIMPLE SUPPERS

Ideal for a light meal, these dishes can be served with crisp, green salads and Continental or farmhouse bread. The pasta meals are quick and easy and all the recipes make good use of everyday ingredients, including varying amounts of garlic.

MEXICAN CHILLI PIE

30 ml (2 tbsp) OIL
1 SPANISH ONION, CHOPPED
3 cloves GARLIC, CRUSHED
450 g (1 lb) COARSE LEAN MINCED BEEF
5 ml (1 tsp) CUMIN
2.5 ml (½ tsp) CHILLI POWDER
150 ml (¼ pint) BEEF STOCK
1 x 400 g (14 oz) CAN CHOPPED TOMATOES
1 GREEN PEPPER, SEEDED AND DICED
15 ml (1 tbsp) TOMATO PURÉE
5 ml (1 tsp) DRIED OREGANO
1 x 440 g (15 ½ oz) CAN MIXED OR RED KIDNEY BEANS, DRAINED

Topping
45 ml (3 tbsp) OLIVE OIL
6 cloves GARLIC, THINLY SLICED
1 SMALL FRENCH STICK, THINLY SLICED
85 g (3 oz) MATURE CHEDDAR CHEESE, FINELY GRATED

Heat the oil in a large pan. Cook the onion until it starts to soften, add the garlic and cook for 2 minutes. Stir in the beef and cook until browned. Add the spices and cook for 1 minute, then stir in the stock, tomatoes, pepper, tomato purée and oregano. Simmer for 25 minutes. Add the beans and season to taste

Heat the oven to 190°C (375°F/Gas mark 5). Transfer the chilli to a large gratin dish. Heat the oil for the topping, add the sliced garlic and cook slowly to soften. Remove from the heat, brush the bread with the oil, and arrange the slices on top of the chilli. Scatter over the slices of garlic and the grated cheese, and bake uncovered for 20 minutes.   SERVES 6

RIGHT: Mexican Chilli Pie

GARLIC AND ONION FLAN

175 g (6 oz) PLAIN FLOUR
45 g (1½ oz) MARGARINE
45 g (1½ oz) WHITE VEGETABLE FAT
25 g (1 oz) BUTTER
450 g (1 lb) ONIONS, THINLY SLICED
1 head GARLIC, ROASTED (SEE PAGE 20)
2 EGGS
150 ml (¼ pint) SINGLE CREAM
60 ml (4 tbsp) MILK
CHOPPED PARSLEY, TO SERVE

Sieve the flour into a bowl with a pinch of salt, add the fats and rub in. Add 30-45 ml (2-3 tbsp) iced water and press the mixture together to form a dough. Lightly knead, then cover and chill for 30 minutes. Pre-heat the oven to 200°C (400°F/Gas mark 6). Roll out the pastry and line a lightly greased 23 cm (9 inch) quiche tin. Prick the base all over. Line the pastry case with a piece of foil and bake for 15 minutes. Remove the foil and cook for a further 5 minutes. Remove from the oven. Reduce the heat to 180°C (350°F/Gas mark 4).

Melt the butter in a large frying pan. Fry the onions for 20 minutes until soft, then remove from the heat. Squeeze the garlic from the skin, mash to a pulp then beat with the eggs, cream and milk. Season. Pour a little into the flan case, add the onions and the remaining egg mixture. Return the flan to the oven on a baking sheet and bake for 30 minutes until the filling is set. Sprinkle with chopped parsley. SERVES 4-6

BROCCOLI AND MUSHROOM RISOTTO

It is important to use Italian arborio rice to achieve the creamy consistency required for a successful risotto.

225 g (8 oz) BROCCOLI, CUT INTO SMALL FLORETS
45 ml (3 tbsp) OLIVE OIL
1 SMALL ONION, FINELY CHOPPED
2 cloves GARLIC, FINELY CHOPPED
300 g (10 oz) RISOTTO (ARBORIO) RICE
150 ml (5 fl oz) DRY WHITE WINE
700 ml (1¼ pint) HOT CHICKEN OR VEGETABLE STOCK
175 g (6 oz) CHESTNUT MUSHROOMS, QUARTERED
55 g (2 oz) FRESHLY GRATED PARMESAN CHEESE
EXTRA PARMESAN CHEESE, TO GARNISH

Cut the broccoli stems into 2.5 cm (1 inch) pieces. Blanch for 2 minutes. Drain. Heat the oil in large pan, add the onion and garlic and cook until golden. Add the rice and cook, stirring until the grains are well coated with oil. Bring the wine and stock to the boil in a separate pan, then add half to the rice and cook for about 10 minutes, stirring until the liquid is absorbed. Add the mushrooms, remaining liquid and cook for a further 10-15 minutes (adding more water if needed) until the rice is tender and the stock absorbed.

Stir in the broccoli and heat for 1-2 minutes. Season. Remove from heat and stir in Parmesan. SERVES 4

TOP: Broccoli and Mushroom Risotto
BOTTOM: Garlic and Onion Flan

SPAGHETTI WITH WALNUT AND PARSLEY SAUCE

3 large cloves GARLIC
45 g (1¹/2 oz) PARSLEY SPRIGS
75 ml (5 tbsp) VIRGIN OLIVE OIL
55 g (2 oz) FRESHLY GRATED PARMESAN CHEESE
55 g (2 oz) WALNUTS, FINELY CHOPPED
75 ml (5 tbsp) SINGLE CREAM
450 g (1 lb) SPAGHETTI OR SPAGHETTINI

PARSLEY AND FRESHLY GRATED PARMESAN
CHEESE TO GARNISH

Put the garlic and parsley in a blender or food processor and blend until finely chopped. Add the oil and blend to make a paste. Turn into a bowl and beat in the Parmesan cheese, walnuts and cream.

Cook the spaghetti in plenty of boiling salted water until *al dente*. Drain well. Return to the pan, add the sauce, toss, then turn into a warmed serving bowl. Garnish with small sprigs of parsley and the extra Parmesan cheese. Serve immediately.   SERVES 4

PANCAKES WITH GARLIC CHEESE FILLING

115 g (4 oz) PLAIN FLOUR
large pinch SALT
2 EGGS
300 ml (¹/2 pint) MILK
30 ml (2 tbsp) CHOPPED PARSLEY OR CHIVES
BUTTER FOR FRYING

Filling
45 g (1¹/2 oz) BUTTER
2 SHALLOTS, FINELY CHOPPED
5 cloves GARLIC, FINELY CHOPPED
225 g (8 oz) RICOTTA CHEESE
115 g (4 oz) MOZZARELLA CHEESE, CHOPPED
25 g (1 oz) FRESHLY GRATED PARMESAN CHEESE

To make 8-10 pancakes, put the flour, salt, eggs and milk into a blender or food processor and blend until smooth. Add the parsley and mix in. Melt a small knob of butter in a 20 cm (8 inch) heavy-based frying pan. Pour in enough batter to coat the base of the pan. Cook the pancake over a medium high heat until set and golden. Turn, and cook the other side until golden. Transfer to a plate or a tray. Continue to make pancakes until all the batter is used up.

Pre-heat the oven to 180°C (350°F/Gas mark 4). Melt 25 g (1 oz) of the butter in a small pan, add the shallots and cook gently for 3 minutes, then add the garlic and cook for 1 minute. Stir into the ricotta cheese with the mozzarella. Place 15 ml (1 tbsp) of the filling at one end of the pancake, fold over the sides, then roll up. Place in an ovenproof dish. Repeat with all the pancakes and filling. Melt the remaining butter and brush the pancakes with it. Scatter over the Parmesan and bake for 12-15 minutes until golden and hot.   SERVES 4

TOP: *Spaghetti with Walnut and Parsley Sauce*
BOTTOM: *Pancakes with Garlic Cheese Filling*

HERB AND GARLIC SOUFFLÉ

If you can find garlic shoots, the young green stems of the plant, use these instead of chives.

115 g (4 oz) CLOVES GARLIC, PEELED
45 g (1¹/2 oz) BUTTER
15 g (¹/2 oz) GRATED PARMESAN CHEESE
55 g (2 oz) PLAIN FLOUR
300 ml (¹/2 pint) WARM MILK
4 EGGS, SEPARATED
5 ml (1 tsp) DIJON MUSTARD
30 ml (2 tbsp) CHOPPED PARSLEY
15 ml (1 tbsp) SNIPPED CHIVES
85 g (3 oz) MATURE CHEDDAR CHEESE, GRATED

Simmer the garlic in water for about 20 minutes until tender. Cool. Press through a sieve to make a pureé. Using 15 g (¹/2 oz) of the butter, grease a 1.4 litre (2¹/2 pint) soufflé dish then coat all over with the Parmesan cheese. Pre-heat oven to 200°C (400°F/Gas mark 6).

Melt the remaining butter in a large heavy saucepan. Blend in the flour and stir over a low heat for 1 minute. Remove from the heat and gradually blend in the milk. Bring to the boil, stirring until thickened. Remove from the heat, beat in the egg yolks, one by one, then add the garlic pureé, mustard, herbs and cheese. Season lightly. Whisk the egg whites until stiff, add a third to the sauce and when fully mixed fold in the rest. Turn into the prepared dish. Reduce the oven temperature to 190°C (375°F/Gas mark 5). Cook for 25 minutes, or until well risen and golden brown. Serve immediately.   SERVES 3-4

GARLIC PIZZA

Using a ready-made pizza base mix saves time and gives a good result.

16 cloves GARLIC
1 x 200g (7 oz) CAN CHOPPED TOMATOES
pinch SUGAR
150 g (5 oz) PACKET PIZZA BASE MIX
25 g (1 oz) CHEDDAR CHEESE, SLICED
25 g (1 oz) GRUYÈRE OR MOZZARELLA CHEESE, SLICED
2.5 ml (¹/2 tsp) DRIED ITALIAN HERBS
15 ml (1 tbsp) OLIVE OIL

Simmer the garlic in water for 10 minutes. Drain. Put the tomatoes in a saucepan with the sugar. Season. Simmer until thick and pulpy. Heat the oven to 220°C (425°F/Gas mark 7). Empty the pizza base mix into a bowl. Chop 6 of the garlic cloves and add to the bowl with 120 ml (4 fl oz) warm water. Knead well on a lightly floured surface for about 5 minutes. Roll out to a diameter of 20 cm (8 inches) and place on a greased baking sheet. Spread over the tomato mixture. Arrange the cheese on top, then scatter over the rest of the garlic, halving any large cloves. Sprinkle over the herbs and oil and bake for 10 minutes. If the top browns too fast, lower the heat to 190°C (375°F/Gas mark 5). Cook for a further 10 minutes until golden brown.   SERVES 2

RIGHT: Garlic Pizza

FRITTATA TRICOLORE

This savoury Mediterranean frittata captures the flavour and colours of a warm climate. Add a little chopped ham, if wished.

45 ml (3 tbsp) OLIVE OIL
1 SPANISH ONION, SLICED
5 cloves GARLIC, SLICED
1 RED PEPPER, SEEDED AND SLICED
1 GREEN PEPPER, SEEDED AND SLICED
8 BLACK OLIVES, PITTED
8 EGGS
15 ml (1 tbsp) CHOPPED PARSLEY
30 ml (2 tbsp) FRESHLY GRATED PARMESAN CHEESE

Heat the oil in a large non-stick frying pan. Add the onion and cook over medium high heat for about 5-6 minutes until it starts to turn golden. Stir in the garlic, peppers and olives and cook for a further 4 minutes, until the peppers begin to soften. Beat the eggs with salt and pepper. Pour into the pan with the parsley, lower the heat and cook for 10-15 minutes until almost set; the top will still be a little runny.

Scatter over the Parmesan, then place under a medium grill until the top is golden. Serve cut into wedges with a green salad. SERVES 4

TAGLIATELLE WITH GARLIC, GORGONZOLA AND BASIL

350 g (12 oz) TAGLIATELLE
55 g (2 oz) BUTTER
3 cloves GARLIC, SLICED
225 g (8 oz) GORGONZOLA CHEESE, CRUMBLED
150 ml (1/4 pint) SINGLE CREAM
30 ml (2 tbsp) CHOPPED BASIL

Bring a large saucepan of salted water to the boil. Add the pasta and boil for 10-12 minutes until *al dente*.

Meanwhile, melt the butter in a pan, add the garlic and cook for 2 minutes. Add half of the Gorgonzola cheese to the pan with the cream, and stir over a low heat until the cheese has melted. Add the basil and season with pepper, if needed. Drain the pasta, divide between warmed serving plates, pour over the sauce and scatter over the remaining Gorgonzola. Serve immediately. SERVES 4

TOP: Frittata Tricolore
BOTTOM: Tagliatelle with Garlic, Gorgonzola and Basil

CARROT AND LENTIL PATTIES

Serve these patties with a refreshing yogurt sauce flavoured with garlic according to taste.

225 g (8 oz) RED LENTILS
15 ml (1 tbsp) OLIVE OIL
1 SMALL ONION, FINELY CHOPPED
225 g (8 oz) CARROTS, VERY FINELY CHOPPED
2 cloves GARLIC, FINELY CHOPPED
10 ml (2 tsp) CUMIN
2.5 ml (1/2 tsp) CAYENNE PEPPER
60 ml (4 tbsp) CHOPPED PARSLEY
55 g (2 oz) FRESH BREADCRUMBS
1 EGG, BEATEN

Sauce
200 g (7 oz) GREEK YOGURT
1-2 cloves GARLIC, CRUSHED
5 ml (1 tsp) LEMON JUICE

Put the lentils in a large pan of salted water, bring to the boil, then simmer for 15 minutes until tender. Drain. Put in a bowl and mash lightly. Heat the oil, add the onion and cook until golden, add the carrots and garlic and cook for a further 3 minutes. Stir in the cumin and cayenne. Add to the lentils, and mix in 45 ml (3 tbsp) of the parsley, breadcrumbs and egg. Season. Shape the mixture into 12 patties, place on a tray and chill until ready to cook.

Combine all the ingredients for the sauce, plus the remaining parsley. Cover and refrigerate until needed.

To cook the patties, brush them on both sides with oil, place on a foil-lined grill pan and cook for about 3-4 minutes on both sides until golden brown, turning carefully. Serve with the yogurt garlic sauce.   MAKES 12

AUBERGINE AND TOMATO BAKE

Passata is sieved tomatoes available in cans, jars or cartons, on sale in most supermarkets. Serve the Aubergine and Tomato Bake cut into slices with salad.

15 ml (1 tbsp) OLIVE OIL, PLUS EXTRA FOR BRUSHING
1 MEDIUM ONION, FINELY CHOPPED
3 large cloves GARLIC, FINELY CHOPPED
450 ml (16 fl oz) PASSATA
7.5 ml (1 1/2 tsp) CHOPPED FRESH THYME OR
2.5 ml (1/2 tsp) DRIED THYME
700 g (1 1/2 lb) AUBERGINES CUT INTO 5 MM
(1/4 INCH) SLICES
2 BEEF STEAK TOMATOES, SKINNED AND THINLY SLICED
85 g (3 oz) FRESHLY GRATED PARMESAN CHEESE

Pre-heat the oven to 180°C (350° F/Gas mark 4). Heat 15 ml (1 tbsp) oil in a frying pan, add the onion and gently cook until soft. Add the garlic and cook for 1 minute. Stir in the passata and thyme and simmer for 10 minutes. Season to taste.

Lightly brush each aubergine slice with oil, and grill on both sides until just golden. Cook in batches. Arrange a layer of these slices, overlapping slightly, in an oiled ovenproof gratin dish. Spoon over one third of the sauce, add a layer of sliced tomato then scatter over 30 ml (2 tbsp) of the cheese. Repeat the layers finishing with aubergine. Brush with oil, then scatter over the rest of the cheese. Cover with foil and bake for 1 1/4 hours.

SERVES 6

TOP: Carrot and Lentil Patties
BOTTOM: Aubergine and Tomato Bake

VEGETABLES

The emphasis of this chapter is on fresh vegetables, which are cooked in various ways to enhance their flavour. All the dishes complement grilled or roasted meats and others, such as Char-roasted Summer Vegetables, can be served as a vegetarian main course.

GARLIC ROSTI

700 g (1 1/2 lb) WAXY POTATOES E.G. WILJA, ROMANO
55 g (2 oz) BUTTER
1 MEDIUM ONION, FINELY CHOPPED
5 cloves GARLIC, FINELY CHOPPED

Peel the potatoes, cut into equal size and boil in salted water for 10 minutes. Drain and cool.

Pre-heat the oven to 190°C (375°F/Gas mark 5). Melt the butter in a large pan, add the onion and cook for 4-5 minutes until it starts to soften. Add the garlic and cook for 1 minute. Coarsely grate the potatoes, (a blender or food processor is very useful here) then stir into the pan, to mix with the onion and garlic. Season to taste. Divide the mixture into 12 and place in patty tins. Bake for 35-40 minutes until crisp and golden. Serve as an accompaniment to roasted meats or poultry.

SERVES 4

BAKED TOMATOES WITH GARLIC CRUMBS

8-12 RIPE FIRM TOMATOES
60 ml (4 tbsp) OLIVE OIL
4 cloves GARLIC, CRUSHED
85 g (3 oz) FINE FRESH WHITE BREADCRUMBS
30 ml (2 tbsp) FRESHLY CHOPPED PARSLEY

Pre-heat the oven to 180°C (350°F/Gas mark 4). Halve the tomatoes and season with salt. Stand them, cut side up, in an ovenproof dish. Heat the oil in a large sauté pan, add the garlic and breadcrumbs and stir over a medium heat for 3-4 minutes until light golden brown. Stir in the parsley then divide between the tomatoes, pressing down slightly. Bake for 25-30 minutes until the tomatoes are soft but still hold their shape and the tops are crisp.

SERVES 4-6

TOP: Garlic Rosti

BOTTOM: Baked Tomatoes with Garlic Crumbs

BRAISED ROOT VEGETABLES WITH GARLIC

30 ml (2 tbsp) OLIVE OIL

25 g (1 oz) BUTTER

1 MEDIUM ONION, QUARTERED

225 g (8 oz) CARROTS, CUT INTO BATONS OF
3.75 CM (1½ INCHES) LONG

225 g (8 oz) PARSNIPS, CUT INTO BATONS OF
3.75 CM (1½ INCHES) LONG

225 g (8 oz) CELERIAC, PEELED AND CUT INTO CHUNKS

350 g (12 oz) SWEDE, CUT INTO CHUNKS

175 g (6 oz) SMALL NEW POTATOES, SCRUBBED

4-6 heads GARLIC

150 ml (¼ pint) VEGETABLE STOCK

Pre-heat the oven to 180°C (350°F/Gas mark 4). Heat the oil and the butter in a large shallow flameproof casserole. Add the vegetables and cook over a high heat until lightly browned. Remove from the heat. Rub off the outside papery skins of the garlic, slice about 1 cm (½ inch) off the tops, and embed them in the vegetables. Season to taste. Add the stock, cover and cook for 45 minutes to 1 hour until the vegetables are tender.

Serve each portion with a head of garlic to be squeezed onto the vegetables while eating.   SERVES 4-6

GARLIC MASHED POTATOES

2 heads GARLIC (ABOUT 20 CLOVES)

700 g (1½ lb) POTATOES, PEELED

55 g (2 oz) BUTTER

Peel the cloves of garlic and put in a large saucepan with the potatoes. Cover with water and boil until soft. Drain (retain the flavoured water for a soup base, if wished). Mash the potatoes with the butter, season with salt and pepper and beat until creamy.   SERVES 4-6

RIGHT: Braised Root Vegetables with Garlic

Green Beans with Garlic

225 g (8 oz) French beans, topped and tailed

25 g (1 oz) butter

3 cloves garlic, finely chopped

juice and rind 1/2 lemon

Halve the beans across the middle. Steam for 5-6 minutes until just tender.

Meanwhile, melt the butter in a small pan, add the garlic and cook gently until light golden Swirl in the lemon juice and rind. Season lightly. Put the beans in a serving dish, pour over the mixture and toss. Any leftovers can be added to a salad the next day. Serves 4

Courgette and Pepper Gratin

1 kg (2 lb) courgettes cut into 0.5 cm (1/4 inch) slices

25 g (1 oz) butter

1 medium onion, sliced

1 large red pepper, seeded and sliced

4 cloves garlic, finely chopped

450 g (1 lb) ripe tomatoes, skinned, seeded and chopped

30 ml (2 tbsp) chopped fresh basil

15 ml (1 tbsp) olive oil

85 g (3 oz) Gruyère cheese, grated

25 g (1 oz) fresh breadcrumbs

Put the courgettes in a large colander, sprinkle with salt and allow to drain for 30 minutes. Rinse and pat dry on kitchen paper.

Pre-heat the oven to 190°C (375°F/Gas mark 5). Melt the butter in a large pan, add the onion and cook until soft and golden. Add the pepper and cook for a further 3 minutes. Stir in the garlic and tomatoes and simmer for about 10 minutes. Stir in the basil and season to taste.

Spread one third of the courgettes on the bottom of a large greased gratin dish, then spoon over half the tomato mixture. Repeat the layers and finish with a layer of courgettes. Brush the top with oil, cover and bake for 45 minutes.

Remove the foil, scatter over the cheese and the breadcrumbs and return to the oven for 15 minutes. Serve with grilled or roast chicken or meat. Serves 6

Top: *Green Beans with Garlic*

Bottom: *Courgette and Pepper Gratin*

CHAR-ROASTED SUMMER VEGETABLES

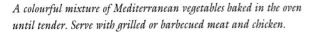

A colourful mixture of Mediterranean vegetables baked in the oven until tender. Serve with grilled or barbecued meat and chicken.

2 MEDIUM COURGETTES, THICKLY SLICED DIAGONALLY

1 MEDIUM AUBERGINE, CUT INTO LARGE CHUNKS

4 SMALL RED ONIONS, HALVED

1 RED PEPPER, SEEDED, CUT INTO LARGE CHUNKS

1 YELLOW PEPPER, SEEDED, CUT INTO LARGE CHUNKS

1 x 400 g (14 oz) CAN ARTICHOKE HALVES, DRAINED AND HALVED

45 ml (3 tbsp) OLIVE OIL

20 cloves GARLIC, PEELED

Put the courgettes and aubergine into a large colander, sprinkle with salt and set aside for 1 hour. Rinse and squeeze them and dry on kitchen paper.

Heat the oven to 230°C (450°F/Gas mark 8). Put all the vegetables in a large shallow baking dish. Drizzle over the olive oil and scatter over the garlic. Toss, and spread the vegetables in a single layer. Bake for 25 minutes until lightly charred.

SERVES 4

GARLIC ROASTED POTATOES

1 kg (2 lb) SMALL NEW POTATOES, SCRUBBED

45 ml (3 tbsp) OLIVE OIL

30 ml (2 tbsp) CHOPPED GARLIC (ABOUT 10 CLOVES)

COARSELY MILLED SEA SALT

Pre-heat the oven to 200°C (400°F/Gas mark 6). Put the potatoes in a pan of cold water, cutting them in half or quarters if more than 7.5 cm (3 inches) in diameter. Bring to the boil and simmer for 5 minutes. Drain well. Heat the oil in a roasting tin in the oven. Add the potatoes and turn in the oil until coated all over, then scatter over the garlic. Roast for approximately 30-35 minutes or until the potatoes are golden and crisp. Season with salt before serving.

SERVES 4-6

RIGHT: Char-roasted Summer Vegetables

OUTDOOR EATING

When the weather is fine, there is no nicer way to eat than *al fresco* and the picnic ideas can be enjoyed without going further than a balcony or the local park. Garlic plays an essential part in the barbecue marinades, infusing meat or vegetables with a mouthwatering flavour.

PARMESAN GARLIC TWISTS
❧

Serve these golden-baked garlic twists at picnics and barbecues.

45 g (1½ oz) BUTTER
3 cloves GARLIC, CRUSHED
250 g (9 oz) PUFF PASTRY, THAWED IF FROZEN
60 ml (4 tbsp) FRESHLY GRATED PARMESAN CHEESE

Pre-heat the oven to 200°C (400°F/Gas mark 6). Melt the butter, add the garlic and cook gently. Roll out the pastry on a floured surface to a rectangle roughly 25 x 35 cm (10 x 14 inches). Brush over two thirds of the garlic butter, then sprinkle with half the cheese. Fold the pastry over from the width; roll again to give a piece 20 x 30 cm (8 x 12 inches). Brush over the remaining garlic butter; scatter over the remaining cheese, pressing down lightly. Cut strips about 5 mm (³/4 inch) wide and 20 cm (8 inches) long. Twist. Place on greased baking trays. Bake for 12 minutes.   MAKES ABOUT 30

CORNMEAL, CHEESE AND GARLIC MUFFINS
❧

5 cloves GARLIC, PEELED
30 ml (2 tbsp) OLIVE OIL
115 g (4 oz) SELF-RAISING FLOUR
15 ml (1 tbsp) BAKING POWDER
1.25 ml (¼ tsp) CAYENNE PEPPER
5 ml (1 tsp) SALT
225 g (8 oz) FINE CORNMEAL OR POLENTA
115 g (4 oz) MATURE CHEDDAR CHEESE, GRATED
55 g (2 oz) BUTTER, MELTED
2 LARGE EGGS, BEATEN
300 ml (½ pint) MILK

Make a garlic purée following the method on page 72 for Herb and Garlic Soufflé. Set aside. Pre-heat the oven to 200°C (400°F/Gas mark 6).

Sift the flour, baking powder, cayenne and salt into a bowl, stir in the cornmeal and cheese. Beat the melted butter, eggs, milk and garlic purée together. Pour onto the dry ingredients and mix quickly until just combined. Spoon the batter into 12 well-greased deep muffin tins and bake in the oven for 20 minutes until risen and golden brown. Cool a few minutes before turning the muffins onto a wire rack to finish cooling.   MAKES 12

TOP: Parmesan Garlic Twists
BOTTOM: Cornmeal, Cheese and Garlic Muffins

TOMATO AND GARLIC TART

Pastry
225 g (8 oz) PLAIN FLOUR
PINCH SALT
1 EGG BEATEN
60 ml (4 tbsp) OLIVE OIL

Filling
60 ml (4 tbsp) OLIVE OIL
450 g (1 lb) ONIONS, THINLY SLICED
1 x 400 g (14 oz) CAN CHOPPED TOMATOES
2.5 ml (½ tsp) DRIED BASIL
2.5 ml (½ tsp) DRIED THYME
pinch DRIED ROSEMARY
6 cloves GARLIC, SLICED
700 g (1½ lb) TOMATOES, SLICED
15 ml (1 tbsp) FRESHLY CHOPPED PARSLEY, TO GARNISH

Put the flour and salt into a bowl. Add the egg, oil and 45 ml (3 tbsp) warm water. Mix well until the mixture forms a dough. Knead on a lightly floured surface, form into a ball, cover with cling film and set aside for 30 minutes.

Roll out the pastry. Grease a 28 cm (11 inch) quiche tin and line it with the pastry. Heat the oven to 200°C (400°F/Gas mark 6). Heat half the oil in a large frying pan, add the onions and cook for about 8 minutes until golden. Add the tomatoes and herbs and cook quickly until the liquid has evaporated. Spoon into the pastry case. Scatter over the garlic. Arrange the tomatoes on top, brush with the remaining oil. Season. Bake for 30 minutes. Reduce the oven temperature to 180°C (350°F/Gas 4) and cook for a further 15 minutes.

Scatter over the parsley and serve. SERVES 8

GARLICKY CHICKEN LIVER PÂTÉ

Smoked chicken or turkey breast is available at delicatessen counters in supermarkets. It adds a slightly smokey flavour to the pâté and gives it a light texture.

450 g (1 lb) CHICKEN LIVERS
55 g (2 oz) BUTTER OR MARGARINE
2 SHALLOTS OR
1 SMALL ONION, SKINNED AND CHOPPED
4 cloves GARLIC, CRUSHED
175 g (6 oz) SMOKED CHICKEN OR TURKEY BREAST
30 ml (2 tbsp) MEDIUM DRY SHERRY
90 ml (6 tbsp) WHIPPING CREAM, WHIPPED

Wash the chicken livers, remove any green pieces, cut in half and dry on kitchen paper. Melt the butter in a frying pan. Add the onion and garlic and cook for about 5 minutes until the onion is softened. Add the chicken livers and cook for about 5 minutes until lightly golden on the outside, but still pink inside. Cool. Transfer to the bowl of a blender or food processor. Add the chicken or turkey breast, the sherry and cream. Purée. Season. Spoon into a dish, level the top, cover and refrigerate. Serve with Melba toast or French bread. SERVES 8

RIGHT: Tomato and Garlic Tart

CROSTINI WITH ROASTED GARLIC PURÉE

❧

Serve crostini as a starter at a barbecue. The bread can be toasted on the grid to give it a smokey flavour.

1 LOAF BREAD E.G. CIABATTA OR BATON
  PAIN DE CAMPAGNE
2 large heads GARLIC, ROASTED (SEE PAGE 20)
30 ml (2 tbsp) OLIVE OIL
150 g (5 oz) SOFT GOAT'S CHEESE
  SMALL BASIL LEAVES, TO GARNISH

Cut the bread into 1.25 cm (^{1}/$_2$ inch) slices and toast lightly on both sides. Squeeze the garlic cloves to remove the soft centres and mix the garlic purée with the oil. Season.

Spread over the toast, top with goat's cheese, then place under the grill to heat through. Garnish with basil leaves and serve.   SERVES 4-6 AS A STARTER OR SNACK

VEGETABLE KEBABS WITH RED PEPPER SALSA

❧

1 LARGE COURGETTE, TOPPED AND TAILED
16 SMALL FIRM TOMATOES
8 CHESTNUT MUSHROOMS
1 GREEN PEPPER, SEEDED AND CUT INTO
  CHUNKS
1 YELLOW OR ORANGE PEPPER, SEEDED
  AND CUT INTO CHUNKS
8 BABY ONIONS, OR *2* SMALL ONIONS,
  QUARTERED

Baste
45 ml (3 tbsp) OLIVE OIL
3 cloves GARLIC, CRUSHED
15 ml (1 tbsp) LEMON JUICE
1.25 ml (¹/₂ tsp) DRIED THYME

Salsa
2 RED PEPPERS, SEEDED AND ROUGHLY
  CHOPPED
45 ml (3 tbsp) OLIVE OIL
3 cloves GARLIC
15 ml (1 tbsp) RED WINE VINEGAR
8 SUN-DRIED TOMATOES IN OIL, DRAINED
1 SMALL RED ONION, ROUGHLY CHOPPED
30 ml (2 tbsp) CHOPPED PARSLEY

Halve the courgette lengthwise and cut into 1.25 cm (^{1}/$_2$ inch) slices. Thread onto skewers with the tomatoes, mushrooms, chunks of pepper and onions. Combine the ingredients for the baste and brush the vegetables.

For the salsa, put the peppers in a blender or food processor with the oil, garlic, vinegar, sun-dried tomatoes and onion. Blend until very finely chopped. Season and add parsley. Cook the kebabs on a prepared barbecue, turning them and brushing with the baste. Serve with the salsa.   SERVES 4

TOP: Crostini with Roasted Garlic Purée
BOTTOM: Vegetable Kebabs with Red Pepper Salsa

BARBECUED RED MULLET WITH SKORDALIÀ

Skordalià is a pungent Greek sauce to serve with fish and vegetables.
A wire basket is useful for cooking a whole fish on a barbecue.

Skordalià

85 g (3 oz)	WHITE BREADCRUMBS
4 cloves	GARLIC
120 ml (8 tbsp)	OLIVE OIL
15 ml (1 tbsp)	WHITE WINE VINEGAR
55 g (2 oz)	GROUND ALMONDS

4 x approx. 200 g (7 oz)	RED MULLET
55 g (2 oz)	BUTTER
1 clove	GARLIC, CRUSHED
15 ml (1 tbsp)	CHOPPED FRESH HERBS

For the skordalià, put the breadcrumbs in a bowl and moisten with water. Crush the garlic with a little salt until pulpy. Squeeze the water from the bread, put in a blender or food processor with the garlic. With the motor running, slowly add the oil, then the vinegar. Turn into a bowl and stir in the ground almonds. (For a thinner sauce add a little lemon juice or single cream).

Wash and scale the fish, cut 2 slashes on each side and season with salt and pepper. Melt the butter and stir in the garlic and herbs. Brush this mixture over the fish. Cook the fish on a prepared barbecue for about 10 minutes, turning to cook them through. Serve with a bowl of the skordalià.   SERVES 4

MEDITERRANEAN LAMB CHOPS

Choose boneless chops or leg steaks if preferred. Serve with green salad.

8	SMALL BONELESS LAMB CHUMP OR LOIN CHOPS

Marinade

6 cloves	GARLIC, CRUSHED
30 ml (2 tbsp)	TOMATO PURÉE
60 ml (4 tbsp)	OLIVE OIL
30 ml (2 tbsp)	RED WINE VINEGAR
10 ml (2 tsp)	PAPRIKA
30 ml (2 tbsp)	CHOPPED ROSEMARY OR MINT
10 ml (2 tsp)	CORIANDER SEEDS, CRUSHED
	FRESH HERBS, TO GARNISH

Put the chops in a glass dish. Mix the ingredients for the marinade, spread half over the chops, turn them over and coat with the rest of the mixture. Cover and refrigate for at least 2 hours or overnight.

Bring to room temperature before cooking. Place the chops on a prepared barbecue and cook for about 15 minutes turning them half way through.   SERVES 4

TOP: Barbecued Red Mullet with Skordalià
BOTTOM: Mediterranean Lamb Chops

SPICY SPARE RIBS

These barbecued ribs are not too spicy so will be popular with children.

1.5 kg (3 lb) AMERICAN STYLE PORK RIBS

Marinade
6-8 cloves GARLIC, CRUSHED
90 ml (6 tbsp) TOMATO KETCHUP
90 ml (6 tbsp) CIDER VINEGAR
60 ml (4 tbsp) SUNFLOWER OIL
15 ml (1 tbsp) WORCESTERSHIRE SAUCE
30 ml (2 tbsp) BROWN SUGAR
10-15 ml (2-3 tsp) CHILLI SAUCE
5 ml (1 tsp) CUMIN
5 ml (1 tsp) DIJON MUSTARD
2.5 ml (1/2 tsp) ALLSPICE

Put the ribs in a large shallow dish. Put all the marinade ingredients in a blender or food processor with 90 ml (6 tbsp) water and blend until smooth. Pour over the ribs and ensure they are all coated with the marinade. Cover and refrigerate for at least 2 hours, preferably overnight. Bring to room temperature before cooking.

Lift from the marinade, place on a prepared barbecue and cook for 25-35 minutes over medium hot coals. Turn the ribs often to prevent burning and brush with the marinade. SERVES 4-6

THAI GARLIC CHICKEN

4 BONELESS CHICKEN BREASTS

Marinade
4 cloves GARLIC, SLICED
15 ml (1 tbsp) FRESH GINGER, FINELY CHOPPED
juice and grated rind 1 LIME
45 ml (3 tbsp) SUNFLOWER OIL
15 ml (1 tbsp) DARK SOY SAUCE
1-2 RED CHILLIES, SEEDED AND THINLY SLICED
30 ml (2 tbsp) CHOPPED FRESH CORIANDER OR
10 ml (2 tbsp) FREEZE-DRIED CORIANDER

Cut 2 or 3 slashes in the chicken skin, put in a glass dish. Mix the ingredients for the marinade, pour over the chicken, cover and refrigerate for at least 2 hours. Bring to room temperature before cooking.

Lift the chicken from the marinade and place on a prepared barbecue, cook over medium hot heat for 15-20 minutes, depending on the size of the chicken breasts. Turn them over and brush with a little marinade to keep them moist. SERVES 4

RIGHT: Thai Garlic Chicken

INDEX